THE ULTIMATE GAP YEAR SURVIVAL GUIDE

Planning and having the best year ever!

Genevieve Velzian

And at the end of the day, your feet should be dirty, your hair messy and your eyes sparkling.

AUTHOR UNKNOWN

INTRODUCTION

So... it's time to talk gap year! Possibly the most exciting thing you'll ever do (perhaps), but equally something you shouldn't put too much pressure on (no one can be non-stop happy for an entire year, trust me!)

I've been there, I've done that, I've spent a year travelling around (Thailand, Vietnam, Cambodia, India, Sri Lanka, Japan, Korea, Malaysia, Indonesia, Australia, America, Canada. I've managed to tick off many other countries on other travels, but these were all in the space of one fantastic year!)

Planning can be considered boring - sure, Jack Kerouac took to the open road with a notebook and a few bottles of dodgy-looking spirits - but sometimes, it's necessary. Having overstayed my visa in Vietnam (and been charged accordingly), and having caught E-Coli (not ideal), and missed a few key vacinnations (hello last minute Rabies jab), please TRUST ME that planning would've helped to prevent nearly all of the annoying bits that I went through.

You don't have to plan everything. You don't need to know exactly where you're going to go, or what you're going to do, or where you're gonna stay, but you do need to know the basics - and this can actually help you to decide on the above (finding out that Phu Quoc was essentially an unlimited visa time-wise, yes please).

So without rambling on too much, let this succinct everything-you-need-to-know guide commence!

1.1 Understanding the Concept

A gap year, traditionally taken between high school and college or during a career break, is a period of time dedicated to personal growth, exploration, and new experiences. This year offers an opportunity to step away from the conventional path and engage in activities that enrich your understanding of the world and yourself. It's a time to explore passions, gain valuable life skills, and see the world from different perspectives.

1.2 Benefits of Taking a Gap Year

Taking a gap year can be transformative in numerous ways. Here are some of the key benefits:

Personal Growth: Stepping out of your comfort zone helps build confidence, independence, and resilience. You'll learn to adapt to new environments, manage challenges, and navigate unfamiliar situations.

Cultural Awareness: Immersing yourself in different cultures broadens your horizons, promotes empathy, and fosters a deeper understanding of global issues. Living and working alongside people from diverse backgrounds can provide invaluable insights and perspectives.

Career Advantages: A well-planned gap year can enhance your CV making you stand out to future employers. Gaining international experience, learning new languages, and developing soft skills such as problem-solving and adaptability are highly valued in today's global job market.

Educational Benefits: Many students return from their gap year with a renewed sense of purpose and clarity about their academic goals. This can lead to improved academic performance and a more focused approach to studies.

1.3 Addressing Common Misconceptions

There are several misconceptions about gap years that can deter people from taking one. Let's address and debunk some of these myths:

"A Gap Year is Just a Year-Long Vacation": While gap years can include travel and leisure, they are far from being a simple vacation. Many participants engage in structured programs, volunteer work, internships, or language courses. These activities provide substantial learning and growth opportunities.

"You'll Fall Behind Your Peers": On the contrary, many who take a gap year return with a clearer sense of direction and motivation, often outperforming peers who went straight to college or continued in their careers without a break. The skills and experiences gained during a gap year can provide a competitive edge.

"It's Too Expensive": While traveling and living abroad can be costly, there are numerous ways to fund a gap year. Scholarships, grants, part-time work, and budget-friendly travel options make it accessible to many. Proper planning and financial management are key.

"It's Risky": Like any significant undertaking, a gap year involves risks. However, with careful planning, research, and preparation, these risks can be minimized. There are many resources and organizations dedicated to supporting gap year participants.

1.4 Conclusion

Taking a gap year is a deeply personal decision that can lead to immense growth and learning. Whether you're looking to explore new cultures, gain work experience, or simply take a break to re-evaluate your goals, a gap year can provide the time and space needed to achieve your aspirations.

The following chapters will guide you through every step of planning, executing, and maximising your gap year, ensuring you make the most of this incredible opportunity.

PLANNING YOUR GAP YEAR

2.1 Setting Goals and Objectives

The first step in planning a successful gap year is to clearly define what you hope to achieve. Goals and objectives will guide your decisions and help you make the most of your time. Consider the following questions:

What are your personal and professional aspirations?

Are you looking to gain work experience, learn a new language, volunteer, travel, or a combination of these?

What skills do you want to develop?

Think about both hard skills (e.g., language proficiency, technical skills) and soft skills (e.g., communication, problem-solving).

How do you want to grow personally? This could include increasing your independence, confidence, and cultural awareness. Even if you're not setting out to actually 'grow' - you just want a fun year abroad - growth is a natural by-product, so you might as well have a think about your current strengths and weaknesses.

Are you shy? Do you struggle to talk to new people? Do you avoid unusual foods? Have you struggled to 'put yourself out there' before, for fear of rejection?

All of these areas can be addressed through travelling, and when I set off I actually had three areas I wanted to push myself in:
1. To meet new people and socialise more.
2. To try new foods, that I'd never tried before.
3. To give myself time to think about what I might want to do as a future career.

When I was having a crappy time, or things weren't going well, it really helped to remind myself of these goals. Even if I was feeling lonely, I could still go and try a new dish or join a surf lesson, thereby ticking off a goal (and getting out of my own mind). Ultimately, I didn't remember the bad feelings as much as the actual experiences I went through - when you've tried tarantula in Cambodia, you don't remember that you were annoyed about the noisy boy in the hostel that very morning.

Create a list of specific, measurable, achievable, relevant, and time-bound (SMART) goals to provide a clear roadmap for your gap year.

2.2 Choosing Your Destinations

Selecting the right destinations is crucial to meeting your gap year goals. Factors to consider include:

Interests and Activities: What activities are available in the region? Look for destinations that offer experiences aligned with your interests.

Language and Culture: Are you interested in learning a new language or immersing yourself in a specific culture?

Safety and Accessibility: Research the safety of potential destinations and consider accessibility, including transportation and visa requirements.

Budget: Some destinations are more budget-friendly than others. Factor in the cost of living, travel, and accommodation.

Popular gap year destinations include countries in Europe, Southeast Asia, South America, and Australia. Each region offers unique experiences and opportunities, but I'll go through each in more detail later in the chapter.

2.3 Budgeting and Financing Your Year

A well-planned budget is essential for a successful gap year. Start by estimating the total cost, including travel, accommodation, food, activities, insurance, and emergency funds. Here are some tips for managing your finances:

Saving: Start saving as early as possible. Consider part-time jobs, freelancing, or selling items you no longer need.

Fundraising: Crowdfunding, sponsorships, and grants can help cover expenses. Look for organisations that offer financial support for gap year participants.

Working Abroad: Many gap year travelers fund their experiences by working part-time jobs or internships abroad. Research work visa requirements and job opportunities in your chosen destinations.

Budgeting Tools: Use budgeting apps and tools to track your expenses and stay on top of your finances.

2.4 Health and Safety Preparations

Ensuring your health and safety while traveling is paramount. Take the following steps to prepare:

Vaccinations and Health Checks: Visit a travel clinic to get necessary vaccinations and health advice for your destinations. Ensure you have a supply of any prescription medications you need.

Travel Insurance: Purchase comprehensive travel insurance that covers medical expenses, trip cancellations, and emergency situations.

Safety Tips: Research the safety of your destinations and learn about any common scams or risks. Register with your embassy or consulate and keep emergency contacts handy.

Packing Essentials: Pack a first aid kit, necessary medications, and travel-sized toiletries. Make copies of important documents (passport, visa, insurance) and keep them in a safe place.

2.5 Creating a Flexible Itinerary

While it's important to have a plan, flexibility is key to a successful gap year. Create a rough itinerary that outlines your major activities and destinations but allows room for spontaneous adventures and changes. Consider the following:

Seasonality: Plan your travel around the best times to visit each destination. Be aware of weather conditions, tourist seasons, and local festivals.

Accommodation and Transportation: Research and book accommodation and transportation in advance for the first few weeks. After that, you can book as you go, allowing for flexibility.

Backup Plans: Have contingency plans in place for emergencies or changes in your itinerary. This might include alternative destinations or activities.

2.6 Final Preparations

As your departure date approaches, finalise your preparations:

Checklists: Use packing and preparation checklists to ensure you don't forget anything important.

Farewells: Spend time with family and friends, and make sure they know how to contact you while you're away.

Mindset: Mentally prepare yourself for the challenges and adventures ahead. Embrace the unknown and be open to new experiences.

By setting clear goals, choosing the right destinations, budgeting wisely, and preparing thoroughly, you'll be well-equipped for a rewarding and successful gap year. The following chapters will delve deeper into the specifics of living abroad, working, volunteering, and making the most of your time away.

WHAT TO PACK

Is this part fun or stressful?

That's for you to decide! I love packing, but then I also pack WAY too much, so it's kinda a case of how minimalist vs maximalist you are.

You can always donate items as you go - I swear there's a whole school in Tanzania wearing the clothes and socks that I left behind (note: if you go to East Africa, many of the people were asking for socks, so it's always wise to pack a few extra pairs).

Packing doesn't have to be a huge deal unless you want it to. You can have a look on YouTube and search for 'what I packed for a year of travel' to get a good idea of what other people have taken, but it should also be specific to you and how big your bag is.

❖ ❖ ❖

Packing for a gap year can be a daunting task, especially when you consider the different climates, activities, and cultural norms you'll encounter. This comprehensive packing guide will help you prepare for your adventure, ensuring you have everything you need while keeping your luggage manageable.

Essential Documents and Items

Before packing anything else, make sure you have the following essential documents and items:

Travel Documents

Passport: Ensure your passport is valid for at least six months beyond your planned return date.

Visas: Check the visa requirements for each country you'll be visiting and obtain the necessary visas in advance.

Travel Insurance: Have a comprehensive travel insurance policy that covers medical emergencies, trip cancellations, and theft.

Copies of Important Documents: Make photocopies of your passport, visas, travel insurance, and other important documents. Store copies separately from the originals and consider keeping digital copies in a secure cloud storage.

Money and Financial Items

Cash: Carry a small amount of cash in the local currency for initial expenses.

Credit/Debit Cards: Bring at least two cards in case one gets lost or stolen. Inform your bank of your travel plans to avoid any issues with transactions.

Travel Wallet: Use a travel wallet to keep your money, cards, and important documents organized and secure.

Health and Safety

Vaccination Records: Carry a copy of your vaccination records, especially if you're traveling to regions that require proof of immunization.

Emergency Contacts: Keep a list of emergency contacts, including family members, your country's embassy, and local emergency numbers.

First Aid Kit: Pack a basic first aid kit with band-aids, antiseptic wipes, pain relievers, and any prescription medications.

Clothing and Footwear

Packing the right clothing and footwear is crucial for staying comfortable and adapting to different climates and activities.

Clothing Basics

T-Shirts and Tank Tops: Pack a mix of short-sleeve and sleeveless tops for warm weather.

Long-Sleeve Shirts: Bring a few long-sleeve shirts for cooler evenings or sun protection.

Sweaters and Hoodies: Pack a lightweight sweater or hoodie for layering in cooler climates.

Jacket: A versatile, weather-resistant jacket is essential. Consider a packable down jacket for cold weather and a waterproof shell for rain.

Pants and Shorts: Bring a mix of lightweight pants, jeans, and shorts. Convertible pants that zip off into shorts can be practical.

Dresses and Skirts: If you wear dresses or skirts, pack a few versatile options that can be dressed up or down.

Undergarments: Pack enough underwear and socks for a week, plus a few extras. Quick-dry materials are ideal for hand-washing on the go.

Sleepwear: Bring comfortable sleepwear suited to the climates you'll be visiting.

Specialty Clothing

Swimwear: Pack at least one swimsuit for beach days, swimming, or water sports.

Activewear: Bring moisture-wicking clothing for hiking, yoga, or other physical activities.

Formal Outfit: Include one slightly dressier outfit for special occasions or nights out.

Footwear

Walking Shoes: Comfortable, sturdy walking shoes or sneakers are essential for everyday use.

Sandals/Flip-Flops: Pack a pair of sandals or flip-flops for the beach, showers, or casual wear.

Hiking Boots: If you plan to do any trekking, bring a pair of supportive hiking boots.

Dress Shoes: Consider bringing a lightweight pair of dress shoes if you anticipate attending formal events.

Toiletries and Personal Care

Keep your toiletries and personal care items to a minimum by focusing on essentials and travel-sized products.

Toiletries

Toothbrush and Toothpaste: A travel toothbrush and small tube of toothpaste.

Shampoo and Conditioner: Travel-sized bottles or solid shampoo bars.

Soap/Body Wash: A small bar of soap or travel-sized body wash.

Deodorant: A compact deodorant stick or roll-on.

Razor: A compact razor and a few spare blades.

Feminine Hygiene Products: Bring a supply of your preferred products, such as tampons, pads, or a menstrual cup.

Hairbrush/Comb: A small, travel-sized hairbrush or comb.

Personal Care

Sunscreen: A high-SPF sunscreen for sun protection.

Insect Repellent: A travel-sized insect repellent, especially for tropical regions.

Hand Sanitizer: A small bottle of hand sanitizer for cleanliness on the go.

Moisturizer: A small, multi-purpose moisturizer for face and body.

Lip Balm: A moisturizing lip balm with SPF.

Contact Lenses and Solution: If you wear contact lenses, bring a sufficient supply and a small bottle of solution.

Prescription Medications: Ensure you have enough of any prescription medications to last your trip, along with copies of your prescriptions.

Electronics and Gadgets

Electronics can enhance your travel experience, but try to limit yourself to essential items to save space and weight.

Communication and Navigation

Smartphone: A smartphone with an international plan or local SIM card for communication and navigation.

Portable Charger: A portable power bank to keep your devices charged on the go.

Travel Adapter: A universal travel adapter for charging your electronics in different countries.

Headphones: Noise-canceling headphones or earbuds for listening to music, podcasts, or audiobooks.

Photography and Entertainment

Camera: A compact digital camera or action camera if you plan to take high-quality photos or videos.

Memory Cards: Extra memory cards for storing photos and videos.

E-Reader/Tablet: An e-reader or tablet for reading, watching movies, or staying connected.

Security and Storage

Laptop: A lightweight laptop if you need to work or stay connected while traveling.

External Hard Drive: An external hard drive for backing up important files and photos.

Locks: A small combination lock for securing your luggage or hostel locker.

Travel Gear and Accessories

Having the right travel gear can make your journey more comfortable and organized.

Luggage

Backpack: A durable, comfortable travel backpack or suitcase that suits your travel style.

Daypack: A smaller daypack or foldable backpack for day trips and excursions.

Packing Cubes: Packing cubes or compression bags to keep your belongings organized and save space.

Dry Bag: A waterproof dry bag for protecting your electronics and valuables from water.

Travel Accessories

Reusable Water Bottle: A reusable water bottle to stay hydrated and reduce plastic waste.

Travel Towel: A quick-dry, compact travel towel.

Laundry Bag: A lightweight, foldable laundry bag for dirty clothes.

Travel Pillow: An inflatable or compressible travel pillow for long flights or bus rides.

Eye Mask and Earplugs: An eye mask and earplugs for better sleep on planes, trains, or in hostels.

Safety and Security

Money Belt: A money belt or hidden pouch for securing your passport, money, and valuables.

RFID Blocker: An RFID-blocking wallet or card holder to protect against electronic theft.

Personal Safety Alarm: A small personal safety alarm for added security.

Seasonal and Destination-Specific Items

Depending on your destinations and the time of year, you may need to pack additional items.

Cold Weather Gear

Thermal Layers: Base layers for added warmth in cold climates.

Gloves, Hat, and Scarf: Warm accessories to protect against the cold.

Winter Coat: A heavy-duty winter coat for extreme cold.

Beach and Tropical Gear

Beach Towel: A lightweight, quick-dry beach towel.

Sunglasses: UV-protective sunglasses.

Sun Hat: A wide-brimmed hat for sun protection.

Adventure and Sports Gear

Hiking Gear: Trekking poles, a hydration pack, and a lightweight tent if you plan to camp.

Snorkeling Gear: A mask and snorkel if you plan to snorkel frequently.

Packing Tips and Tricks

Here are some tips to help you pack efficiently and make the most of your luggage space.

Roll, Don't Fold

Rolling your clothes instead of folding them can save space and reduce wrinkles.

Layering

Plan your wardrobe around layering. This will give you more outfit combinations and help you adapt to varying climates.

Limit Shoes

Shoes can take up a lot of space and weight. Try to limit yourself to 2-3 pairs that cover all your needs.

Multi-Use Items

Pack items that have multiple uses, such as a sarong that can serve as a beach cover-up, a scarf, or a blanket.

Pack Light

Remember that you can often buy things you need along the way. Packing light will make your travels easier and more enjoyable.

Conclusion

Packing for a gap year is all about finding the right balance between being prepared and packing light. Focus on versatile, high-quality items that will serve you well in various situations. Use this guide to help you pack efficiently and ensure you have everything you need for a safe, comfortable, and enjoyable adventure.

This detailed packing guide will help you prepare for your gap year, ensuring you have everything you need to make the most of your journey while keeping your luggage manageable (note: not falling over on a beach in front of everyone because your rucksack is too heavy, a la me).

DESTINATIONS IN MORE DETAIL

I promised you more detail about places to go, and here I deliver! You're likely to meet people on your travels who ultimately influence where you go (it's nice to travel with other people sometimes), but all the same, there might be a few places on your bucket list that you absolutely have to tick off.

Here are some popular destinations and a bit more detail about each one.

1. Southeast Asia

Southeast Asia is a fav
orite destination for gap year travelers due to its affordability, diverse cultures, and stunning landscapes.

1.1 Thailand

Bangkok: A bustling metropolis known for its vibrant street life, ornate temples, and rich history.

Chiang Mai: A city in the mountainous north, famous for its temples, night markets, and opportunities for trekking and volunteering with elephants.

Islands: Koh Phi Phi, Koh Samui, and Phuket offer idyllic beaches, snorkeling, and vibrant nightlife.

1.2 Vietnam

Hanoi and Ho Chi Minh City: Experience the contrasting atmospheres of the old capital and the bustling southern metropolis. Dare I say that I prefer the southern city - Ho Chi Minh is one of my favourite places - but both are absolutely must-visits on your journey!

Ha Long Bay: Cruise through the stunning karst limestone formations and emerald waters. If you can afford to, an overnight boat trip is highly recommended.

Hoi An: A charming town known for its preserved Ancient Town, lantern-lit streets, and tailor shops. I spent a month in Hoi An and absolutely loved it, but some other travellers found it far too sleepy and left after a few days. It depends what you're looking for!

1.3 Cambodia

Siem Reap and Angkor Wat: Explore the ancient temples of Angkor Wat, a UNESCO World Heritage site. I've been twice now and I just can't get enough of the incredible history and that feeling of being a tiny ant in a big universe.

Phnom Penh: Visit the capital to learn about Cambodia's history, including the sobering Tuol Sleng Genocide Museum.

1.4 Indonesia

Bali: Known for its beaches, rice terraces, and vibrant culture. Having spent many months here over the years, it's safe to say that this is one of my all-time favourite countries! Hit up Kuta for the nightlife, but make sure to visit Ubud and the more traditional places too. If anything, none of your social media contacts want to see a zillion pictures of you in a nightclub - get some cultural pics too...

Yogyakarta: Home to the ancient temples of Borobudur and Prambanan.

2. Europe

Europe offers a wealth of history, culture, and diverse experiences, making it an ideal gap year destination.

2.1 Spain

Barcelona: Famous for its architecture by Gaudí, lively streets, and beautiful beaches.

Madrid: Spain's capital, known for its museums, parks, and nightlife.

Granada: Home to the stunning Alhambra palace.

2.2 Italy

Rome: Explore ancient ruins, Vatican City, and world-class museums.

Florence: The heart of the Renaissance with incredible art and architecture.

Venice: Known for its canals, historic buildings, and romantic ambiance.

2.3 France

Paris: The city of lights, known for its art, fashion, and iconic landmarks like the Eiffel Tower and Louvre Museum.

Provence: Experience the picturesque countryside, lavender fields, and charming villages.

2.4 Eastern Europe

Prague, Czech Republic: A city of stunning Gothic architecture and vibrant nightlife. Super cheap beer, if that's your thing, and the most stunning architecture.

Budapest, Hungary: Known for its thermal baths, historic sites, and beautiful Danube River views.

Croatia: Explore the Dalmatian Coast, including the cities of Dubrovnik and Split, and the stunning Plitvice Lakes.

3. South America

South America offers diverse landscapes, vibrant cultures, and countless adventures.

3.1 Peru

Machu Picchu: Trek the Inca Trail to this iconic archaeological site.

Cusco: The historical capital of the Inca Empire, with rich history and culture.

Amazon Rainforest: Explore the biodiversity and indigenous cultures of the Amazon.

3.2 Brazil

Rio de Janeiro: Famous for its Carnival, Christ the Redeemer statue, and beautiful beaches.

Iguaçu Falls: One of the largest and most impressive waterfall systems in the world.

3.3 Argentina

Buenos Aires: Known for its European-style architecture, tango music, and vibrant cultural scene.

Patagonia: A region of stunning natural beauty, perfect for trekking and outdoor adventures.

4. Oceania

Australia and New Zealand offer incredible landscapes, outdoor activities, and unique wildlife.

4.1 Australia

Sydney: Home to the iconic Sydney Opera House and beautiful beaches like Bondi.

Great Barrier Reef: The world's largest coral reef system, ideal for diving and snorkeling.

Melbourne: Known for its artsy vibe, coffee culture, and laneways.

4.2 New Zealand

Auckland: A vibrant city with beautiful harbours and islands.

Queenstown: The adventure capital, offering activities like bungee jumping, skiing, and hiking.

Rotorua: Known for its geothermal activity and Maori culture.

5. Africa

Africa is a continent of vast landscapes, rich cultures, and extraordinary wildlife experiences.

5.1 South Africa

Cape Town: Known for its stunning scenery, Table Mountain, and cultural diversity.

Kruger National Park: One of Africa's largest game reserves, offering incredible safari experiences.

5.2 Tanzania

Serengeti National Park: Famous for its annual migration of over 1.5 million wildebeest and 250,000 zebras. I did a G-Adventures 21-day tour through several African countries, and the Serengeti was a top highlight - there's really nothing like it.

Zanzibar: An archipelago with beautiful beaches and a rich history. Possibly the most stunning place you'll go in your whole year - the beaches are crystal clear waters and proper white sand here. It's not a wild nightlife hub - as you have to be quite careful here - so it would best suit someone who's looking for cultural exploration over all-night parties.

<u>5.3 Morocco</u>

Marrakech: Known for its bustling souks, historic medinas, and stunning palaces.

Sahara Desert: Experience the vast sand dunes and traditional Berber culture.

6. North America

North America offers a diverse range of experiences, from vibrant cities to stunning national parks.

<u>6.1 United States</u>

New York City: The city that never sleeps, known for its iconic landmarks, museums, and cultural diversity.

California: Explore cities like San Francisco and Los Angeles, as well as natural wonders like Yosemite National Park.

National Parks: Yellowstone, Grand Canyon, and Zion offer some of the most breathtaking landscapes.

7. Canada

Vancouver: A coastal city known for its natural beauty and outdoor activities.

Banff National Park: Famous for its stunning mountain scenery, turquoise lakes, and abundant wildlife.

Toronto: A vibrant and diverse city with cultural landmarks and a bustling food scene.

ASIA

Asia deserves its very own additional chapter, as it's often the continent on every gap yearee's lips!

There are so many fantastic places to visit in Asia, and they're often low-cost, which means you can travel for longer. Having travelled through America, and separately South East Asia, I can confirm that you'll spend 10x more in the States and likely have to cut your trip short! Not ideal.

While you might be off on a shorter jaunt, say a few months, and can make the most of spending time in places like New York and San Francisco, for the vast majority of gap yearees, it's a case of trying to find somewhere with £1/ $1 noodles, £1/ $1 drinks, and the ability to veg out on a beach beanbag when things get too much or too overwhelming.

That means that Asia is a fantastic place to spend some real time - especially because there's a bit of a gap year 'circuit' that everyone does, and you'll find that you constantly bump into the same people over and over again.

I met people in Ho Chi Minh that I bumped into on Koh Rong island and then again on Koh Mak island - it was a bizarre turn of events! But that's just the mood - you get to know certain faces and then you see them everywhere.

So, let's crack on with more detail on places to hit in Asia.

Asia is a continent of incredible diversity, offering a myriad of cultures, landscapes, cuisines, and experiences. From bustling metropolises to serene temples, lush jungles to arid deserts, there's something for every type of traveler. In this chapter, we'll explore the top destinations in Asia to visit on your gap year, highlighting must-see sights, activities, and tips for each location.

1. Japan

Japan seamlessly blends ancient traditions with cutting-edge technology, offering a unique and enriching travel experience.

1.1 Tokyo

Shibuya Crossing: Experience the world's busiest pedestrian crossing in Shibuya, a vibrant area known for its shopping, dining, and entertainment.

Asakusa and Sensō-ji Temple: Visit the historic Asakusa district and the iconic Sensō-ji Temple, the oldest temple in Tokyo.

Tokyo Skytree: Get panoramic views of the city from the Tokyo Skytree, one of the tallest towers in the world.

1.2 Kyoto

Fushimi Inari Shrine: Walk through the thousands of red torii gates at this famous Shinto shrine.

Kinkaku-ji (Golden Pavilion): Marvel at the stunning golden temple surrounded by beautiful gardens.

Arashiyama Bamboo Grove: Stroll through the enchanting bamboo forest in Arashiyama.

1.3 Osaka

Dotonbori: Explore the lively Dotonbori area, known for its neon lights, street food, and entertainment.

Osaka Castle: Visit the historic Osaka Castle, surrounded by picturesque gardens.

Universal Studios Japan: Spend a fun-filled day at this popular theme park.

1.4 Hiroshima

Hiroshima Peace Memorial Park: Reflect on history at the Peace Memorial Park and Museum, dedicated to the victims of the atomic bomb.

Miyajima Island: Take a ferry to Miyajima Island and see the iconic floating torii gate at Itsukushima Shrine.

1.5 Tips for Traveling in Japan

Rail Pass: Consider purchasing a Japan Rail Pass for unlimited travel on JR trains, including the Shinkansen (bullet trains).

Language: Learn some basic Japanese phrases to help with communication, as English is not widely spoken.

Etiquette: Familiarize yourself with Japanese customs and etiquette, such as bowing, removing shoes before entering homes, and the importance of politeness.

2. Thailand
Thailand, known as the Land of Smiles, is famous for its beautiful beaches, rich culture, and delicious cuisine.

2.1 Bangkok

Grand Palace and Wat Phra Kaew: Visit the opulent Grand Palace and the Temple of the Emerald Buddha.

Wat Arun: Climb the steps of Wat Arun, also known as the Temple of Dawn, for a stunning view of the Chao Phraya River.

Chatuchak Weekend Market: Shop for souvenirs, clothes, and local delicacies at one of the world's largest markets.

2.2 Chiang Mai

Old City Temples: Explore the ancient temples in the Old City, including Wat Phra Singh and Wat Chedi Luang.

Elephant Sanctuaries: Visit ethical elephant sanctuaries where you can learn about and interact with rescued elephants.

Doi Suthep: Hike or drive up to Doi Suthep and visit Wat Phra That Doi Suthep, offering panoramic views of the city.

2.3 Phuket

Patong Beach: Experience the vibrant nightlife and beautiful beaches in Patong.

Phang Nga Bay: Take a boat tour to see the stunning limestone karsts and emerald waters of Phang Nga Bay.

Big Buddha: Visit the Big Buddha, a massive statue overlooking the island.

2.4 Krabi

Railay Beach: Relax on the picturesque Railay Beach, accessible only by boat.

Phi Phi Islands: Take a day trip to the Phi Phi Islands, famous for their crystal-clear waters and vibrant marine life.

Hot Springs and Emerald Pool: Enjoy the natural hot springs and swim in the clear waters of the Emerald Pool.

2.5 Tips for Traveling in Thailand

Weather: Be aware of the rainy season (May to October) and plan your travels accordingly.

Local Transport: Use tuk-tuks and songthaews (shared taxis) for short distances, and consider renting a scooter for more flexibility.

Cultural Sensitivity: Dress modestly when visiting temples and respect local customs and traditions.

3. Vietnam

Vietnam offers a rich tapestry of history, culture, and natural beauty, from bustling cities to serene countryside.

3.1 Hanoi

Old Quarter: Wander through the narrow streets of the Old Quarter, filled with shops, cafes, and street food vendors.

Hoan Kiem Lake: Relax by Hoan Kiem Lake and visit Ngoc Son Temple on its small island.

Ho Chi Minh Mausoleum: Pay respects at the mausoleum of Ho Chi Minh, Vietnam's revered leader.

3.2 Ha Long Bay

Boat Cruise: Take an overnight boat cruise through Ha Long Bay, famous for its emerald waters and limestone islands.

Kayaking and Caving: Explore the bay's hidden caves and lagoons by kayak.

3.3 Hoi An

Ancient Town: Stroll through the well-preserved Ancient Town, a UNESCO World Heritage site, known for its lantern-lit streets and historic architecture.

Tailor Shops: Get custom-made clothing at one of Hoi An's many tailor shops.

Cua Dai Beach: Relax on the sandy shores of Cua Dai Beach, just a short bike ride from the town center.

3.4 Ho Chi Minh City (Saigon)

War Remnants Museum: Learn about the Vietnam War and its impact at this powerful museum.

Cu Chi Tunnels: Explore the Cu Chi Tunnels, an extensive underground network used during the Vietnam War.

Ben Thanh Market: Shop for souvenirs and sample local foods at this bustling market.

3.5 Sapa

Trekking: Trek through the terraced rice fields and hill tribe villages of Sapa.

Fansipan Mountain: Climb or take a cable car to the summit of Fansipan, the highest peak in Indochina.

3.6 Tips for Traveling in Vietnam

Currency: Use Vietnamese Dong (VND) and carry small bills for street vendors and small shops.

Local Cuisine: Don't miss trying pho (noodle soup), banh mi (Vietnamese sandwich), and fresh spring rolls.

Transport: Consider using overnight trains and buses to save on accommodation costs and maximize your time.

4. India

India is a land of contrasts, offering a rich tapestry of cultures, traditions, and landscapes.

4.1 Delhi

Red Fort: Visit the historic Red Fort, a UNESCO World Heritage site.

Qutub Minar: Explore the Qutub Minar complex, home to India's tallest minaret.

India Gate: Take a stroll around India Gate, a war memorial located in the heart of New Delhi.

4.2 Agra

Taj Mahal: Witness the beauty of the Taj Mahal, one of the Seven Wonders of the World.

Agra Fort: Explore the impressive Agra Fort, another UNESCO World Heritage site.

4.3 Jaipur

Amber Fort: Visit the stunning Amber Fort, located on a hilltop overlooking Maota Lake.

City Palace: Explore the City Palace, a complex of courtyards, gardens, and buildings in the heart of Jaipur.

Hawa Mahal: Admire the intricate facade of Hawa Mahal, also known as the Palace of Winds.

4.4 Varanasi

Ganges River: Witness the daily rituals and ceremonies on the ghats (steps) of the Ganges River.

Sarnath: Visit Sarnath, the site where Buddha delivered his first sermon after attaining enlightenment.

4.5 Kerala

Backwaters: Take a houseboat cruise through the serene backwaters of Kerala.

Munnar: Visit the hill station of Munnar, known for its tea plantations and scenic beauty.

Kochi: Explore the historic city of Kochi, with its colonial architecture and vibrant arts scene.

4.6 Tips for Traveling in India

Dress Modestly: Respect local customs by dressing modestly, especially when visiting religious sites.

Health Precautions: Be cautious with street food and drink only bottled or filtered water.

Transport: Use trains for long-distance travel and auto-rickshaws for short distances. Pre-book tickets for popular routes to ensure availability.

5. Indonesia

Indonesia is an archipelago of over 17,000 islands, offering diverse landscapes, cultures, and experiences.

5.1 Bali

Ubud: Explore the cultural heart of Bali, known for its arts, crafts, and wellness retreats.

Tegallalang Rice Terraces: Visit the picturesque Tegallalang Rice Terraces for a glimpse of Bali's traditional agriculture.

Uluwatu Temple: Watch the sunset over the ocean from Uluwatu Temple, perched on a cliff.

5.2 Yogyakarta

Borobudur: Visit Borobudur, the world's largest Buddhist temple and a UNESCO World Heritage site.

Prambanan: Explore Prambanan, a 9th-century Hindu temple complex.

Kraton Palace: Visit the Kraton, the Sultan's palace in Yogyakarta.

5.3 Komodo National Park

Komodo Dragons: See the world's largest lizards, the Komodo dragons, in their natural habitat.

Diving and Snorkeling: Discover the vibrant marine life and coral reefs around the park's islands.

5.4 Lombok

Mount Rinjani: Trek to the summit of Mount Rinjani, Indonesia's second-highest volcano.

Gili Islands: Relax on the Gili Islands, known for their white sandy beaches and clear waters.

5.5 Tips for Traveling in Indonesia

Respect Local Customs: Dress modestly and be mindful of local customs, especially in more conservative areas.

Transport: Use ferries and flights to travel between islands, and rent a scooter for exploring locally.

Safety: Be cautious when swimming or diving, as currents can be strong in some areas.

6. China

China offers a vast array of historical, cultural, and natural attractions, from ancient landmarks to modern cities.

6.1 Beijing

Great Wall of China: Visit the Great Wall, one of the most iconic landmarks in the world. Popular sections include Badaling, Mutianyu, and Jinshanling.

Forbidden City: Explore the Forbidden City, the imperial palace of the Ming and Qing dynasties.

Temple of Heaven: Visit the Temple of Heaven, a complex of religious buildings used for ceremonies by emperors.

6.2 Shanghai

The Bund: Stroll along the Bund, Shanghai's famous waterfront promenade, and admire the colonial-era architecture.

Yu Garden: Explore Yu Garden, a classical Chinese garden in the heart of the city.

Shanghai Tower: Get a bird's-eye view of the city from the observation deck of Shanghai Tower, the second-tallest building in the world.

6.3 Xi'an

Terracotta Army: Visit the Terracotta Army, an incredible archaeological site with thousands of life-sized statues of soldiers and horses.

City Wall: Walk or bike along the ancient city wall of Xi'an, one of the best-preserved city walls in China.

Muslim Quarter: Explore the bustling Muslim Quarter, known for its street food and vibrant markets.

6.4 Guilin and Yangshuo

Li River Cruise: Take a boat cruise along the Li River, famous for its stunning karst landscape.

Longji Rice Terraces: Visit the Longji Rice Terraces, also known as the Dragon's Backbone, for breathtaking views and hiking opportunities.

Yangshuo: Explore the town of Yangshuo, known for its outdoor activities such as rock climbing, cycling, and caving.

6.5 Chengdu

Giant Panda Research Base: See giant pandas up close at the Chengdu Research Base of Giant Panda Breeding.

Jinli Ancient Street: Stroll through Jinli Ancient Street, known for its traditional architecture, shops, and street food.

Leshan Giant Buddha: Take a day trip to see the Leshan Giant Buddha, the largest stone Buddha statue in the world.

6.6 Tips for Traveling in China

Visa Requirements: Ensure you have the necessary visa and permits for your travels in China.

Language Barrier: Learn basic Mandarin phrases or use translation apps to help with communication.

Transport: Use high-speed trains for efficient travel between major cities, and consider booking tickets in advance.

7. South Korea

South Korea is a vibrant country known for its rich history, modern cities, and delicious cuisine.

7.1 Seoul

Gyeongbokgung Palace: Visit Gyeongbokgung Palace, the largest and most iconic of the Five Grand Palaces.

Bukchon Hanok Village: Explore Bukchon Hanok Village, a traditional Korean village with preserved hanok houses.

Myeongdong: Shop and eat your way through Myeongdong, a bustling shopping district known for its street food.

7.2 Busan

Haeundae Beach: Relax on Haeundae Beach, one of South Korea's most famous beaches.

Gamcheon Culture Village: Wander through Gamcheon Culture Village, known for its colorful houses and street art.

Jagalchi Fish Market: Visit Jagalchi Fish Market, the largest seafood market in Korea.

7.3 Jeju Island

Hallasan National Park: Hike to the summit of Hallasan, South Korea's highest mountain.

Seongsan Ilchulbong: Climb Seongsan Ilchulbong, also known as Sunrise Peak, for stunning views of the island.

Jeju Loveland: Explore Jeju Loveland, a unique outdoor sculpture park.

7.4 Gyeongju

Bulguksa Temple: Visit Bulguksa Temple, a UNESCO World Heritage site and one of Korea's most important Buddhist temples.

Seokguram Grotto: Explore Seokguram Grotto, an artificial cave temple with a large stone Buddha.

Anapji Pond: Walk around Anapji Pond, a beautiful garden and palace complex from the Silla Dynasty.

7.5 Tips for Traveling in South Korea

Public Transport: Use the efficient and extensive public transport system, including subways, buses, and high-speed trains.

Technology: Take advantage of free Wi-Fi available in many public places, and use apps like KakaoMap for navigation.

Cultural Etiquette: Learn about Korean customs and etiquette, such as bowing and removing shoes before entering homes.

8. Nepal

Nepal is a paradise for trekkers and nature lovers, offering stunning landscapes, rich culture, and spiritual experiences.

8.1 Kathmandu

Swayambhunath (Monkey Temple): Visit Swayambhunath, an ancient stupa known for its panoramic views of Kathmandu and resident monkeys.

Pashupatinath Temple: Explore Pashupatinath, one of the holiest Hindu temples in the world.

Durbar Square: Wander through Kathmandu Durbar Square, a historic area with palaces, courtyards, and temples.

8.2 Pokhara

Phewa Lake: Relax by Phewa Lake and enjoy boating with views of the Annapurna mountain range.

World Peace Pagoda: Hike up to the World Peace Pagoda for stunning views of Pokhara and the Himalayas.

Paragliding: Experience the thrill of paragliding over Pokhara, one of the best paragliding spots in the world.

8.3 Annapurna Region

Annapurna Circuit: Trek the Annapurna Circuit, one of the most popular long-distance treks in the world, offering diverse landscapes and cultural experiences.

Annapurna Base Camp: Hike to Annapurna Base Camp, surrounded by towering peaks and glaciers.

8.4 Everest Region

Everest Base Camp Trek: Take on the challenge of trekking to Everest Base Camp, with breathtaking views of the world's highest peak.

Namche Bazaar: Visit Namche Bazaar, a bustling Sherpa town and acclimatization stop on the Everest trail.

8.5 Chitwan National Park

Wildlife Safari: Go on a wildlife safari in Chitwan National Park to see rhinos, tigers, elephants, and more.

Canoeing and Bird Watching: Enjoy canoeing on the Rapti River and bird watching in the park.

8.6 Tips for Traveling in Nepal

Permits: Obtain necessary trekking permits (TIMS and ACAP/MCAP) for popular trekking routes.

Altitude Sickness: Acclimatize properly and be aware of the symptoms of altitude sickness when trekking at high altitudes.

Respect Local Culture: Dress modestly, especially in rural areas and religious sites, and respect local customs and traditions.

9. Cambodia

Cambodia is a country rich in history and natural beauty, with ancient temples, bustling cities, and pristine beaches.

9.1 Siem Reap

Angkor Wat: Visit Angkor Wat, the largest religious monument in the world and a UNESCO World Heritage site.

Angkor Thom and Bayon Temple: Explore Angkor Thom, the ancient capital city, and its iconic Bayon Temple with its smiling stone faces.

Ta Prohm: Discover Ta Prohm, a temple overgrown with trees and roots, famously featured in the movie "Tomb Raider."

9.2 Phnom Penh

Royal Palace: Visit the Royal Palace, the official residence of the King of Cambodia.

Tuol Sleng Genocide Museum: Learn about Cambodia's tragic history at the Tuol Sleng Genocide Museum.

Choeung Ek (Killing Fields): Pay your respects at Choeung Ek, one of the many Killing Fields from the Khmer Rouge regime.

9.3 Sihanoukville

Otres Beach: Relax on the beautiful Otres Beach, known for its clear waters and laid-back atmosphere.

Koh Rong: Take a ferry to Koh Rong, an island paradise with white sandy beaches and vibrant marine life.

9.4 Battambang

Bamboo Train: Experience the unique Bamboo Train ride through the countryside.

Phnom Sampeau: Visit Phnom Sampeau, a hilltop temple complex with stunning views and historical significance.

9.5 Kampot and Kep

Kampot: Explore the charming riverside town of Kampot, known for its pepper farms and colonial architecture.

Kep: Visit Kep, a seaside town famous for its crab market and nearby Kep National Park.

9.6 Tips for Traveling in Cambodia

Currency: Use both Cambodian Riel (KHR) and US dollars (USD) for transactions.

Transport: Use tuk-tuks for short distances and buses or private cars for longer journeys.

Respect Local Customs: Dress modestly, especially when visiting temples, and be mindful of cultural norms.

10. Sri Lanka

Sri Lanka is a gem in the Indian Ocean, offering diverse landscapes, rich history, and warm hospitality.

10.1 Colombo

Gangaramaya Temple: Visit Gangaramaya Temple, one of the most important Buddhist temples in Colombo.

Galle Face Green: Stroll along Galle Face Green, a popular oceanfront park.

Pettah Market: Explore Pettah Market, a bustling bazaar with a wide range of goods.

10.2 Kandy

Temple of the Tooth: Visit the Temple of the Tooth, a UNESCO World Heritage site and one of the most sacred Buddhist sites in Sri Lanka.

Kandy Lake: Walk around Kandy Lake, a serene body of water in the heart of the city.

Royal Botanic Gardens: Explore the Royal Botanic Gardens in Peradeniya, known for its extensive collection of plants.

10.3 Ella

Nine Arches Bridge: See the iconic Nine Arches Bridge, a beautiful colonial-era railway bridge.

Little Adam's Peak: Hike to Little Adam's Peak for stunning views of the surrounding countryside.

Ella Rock: Challenge yourself with a hike to Ella Rock, offering panoramic views of the region.

10.4 Sigiriya

Sigiriya Rock Fortress: Climb Sigiriya, an ancient rock fortress with breathtaking views and fascinating history.

Pidurangala Rock: Hike Pidurangala Rock for an alternative view of Sigiriya and the surrounding landscape.

10.5 Galle

Galle Fort: Explore Galle Fort, a UNESCO World Heritage site with colonial-era architecture and charming streets.

Unawatuna Beach: Relax on Unawatuna Beach, known for its clear waters and laid-back vibe.

10.6 Yala National Park

Wildlife Safari: Go on a safari in Yala National Park to see leopards, elephants, and a variety of other wildlife.

10.7 Tips for Traveling in Sri Lanka

Transport: Use trains for scenic journeys and tuk-tuks for short distances. Private cars and buses are also available for longer trips.

Cultural Sensitivity: Dress modestly and respect local customs, especially when visiting religious sites.

Weather: Be aware of the monsoon seasons (May to September in the southwest and October to February in the northeast) and plan your travels accordingly.

11. Malaysia

Malaysia offers a mix of modern cities, cultural heritage, and natural beauty, making it a diverse travel destination.

11.1 Kuala Lumpur

Petronas Twin Towers: Visit the Petronas Twin Towers, the tallest twin towers in the world, and enjoy the view from the observation deck.

Batu Caves: Explore Batu Caves, a limestone hill with a series of caves and temples.

Merdeka Square: Visit Merdeka Square, a historic site where Malaysia declared independence.

11.2 Penang

George Town: Wander through George Town, a UNESCO World Heritage site known for its colonial architecture and vibrant street art.

Penang Hill: Take the funicular railway up Penang Hill for panoramic views of the island.

Street Food: Sample Penang's famous street food, including char kway teow, laksa, and cendol.

11.3 Langkawi

Beaches: Relax on the pristine beaches of Langkawi, known for their white sand and clear waters.

Langkawi Sky Bridge: Walk across the Langkawi Sky Bridge for stunning views of the surrounding islands and rainforest.

Island Hopping: Take a boat tour to explore the nearby islands and marine parks.

11.4 Borneo (Sabah and Sarawak)

Mount Kinabalu: Climb Mount Kinabalu, the highest peak in Southeast Asia.

Sepilok Orangutan Rehabilitation Centre: Visit the Sepilok Orangutan Rehabilitation Centre to see rescued orangutans up close.

Bako National Park: Explore Bako National Park, known for its wildlife, including proboscis monkeys, and diverse ecosystems.

11.5 Malacca

Jonker Street: Stroll along Jonker Street, known for its antique shops, cafes, and vibrant night market.

A Famosa: Visit A Famosa, the remains of a Portuguese fort built in the 16th century.

St. Paul's Hill: Climb St. Paul's Hill for views of the city and visit the historic St. Paul's Church.

11.6 Tips for Traveling in Malaysia

Language: English is widely spoken, making it easy to communicate with locals.

Transport: Use buses and trains for intercity travel, and consider renting a car for more flexibility in exploring rural areas.

Respect Local Customs: Dress modestly and respect local customs, especially in religious and rural areas.

12. Philippines

The Philippines is an archipelago of over 7,000 islands, offering beautiful beaches, vibrant cities, and unique cultural experiences.

12.1 Manila

Intramuros: Explore Intramuros, the historic walled city of Manila, with its colonial architecture and historic sites.

Rizal Park: Visit Rizal Park, a large urban park dedicated to the national hero, José Rizal.

Binondo: Explore Binondo, the world's oldest Chinatown, known for its food and cultural heritage.

12.2 Palawan

El Nido: Discover the stunning lagoons, beaches, and limestone cliffs of El Nido.

Puerto Princesa Subterranean River: Take a boat tour of the Puerto Princesa Subterranean River, a UNESCO World Heritage site.

Coron: Dive in the crystal-clear waters of Coron, known for its shipwrecks and vibrant coral reefs.

12.3 Cebu

Kawasan Falls: Swim in the turquoise waters of Kawasan Falls, a series of beautiful waterfalls and natural pools.

Oslob: Experience the thrill of swimming with whale sharks in Oslob.

Sirao Flower Garden: Visit Sirao Flower Garden, known as the "Little Amsterdam" of Cebu, for its colorful flower fields.

12.4 Bohol

Chocolate Hills: See the unique Chocolate Hills, a geological formation of over 1,200 grassy hills that turn brown in the dry season.

Tarsier Sanctuary: Visit the Tarsier Sanctuary to see the world's smallest primates, the Philippine tarsiers.

Panglao Island: Relax on the beaches of Panglao Island, known for its white sand and clear waters.

12.5 Siargao

Surfing: Surf the famous Cloud 9 waves in Siargao, known as the surfing capital of the Philippines.

Island Hopping: Explore nearby islands such as Naked Island, Daku Island, and Guyam Island.

Magpupungko Rock Pools: Visit the Magpupungko Rock Pools, natural tidal pools perfect for swimming and snorkeling.

12.6 Tips for Traveling in the Philippines

Island Hopping: Plan your travels to include multiple islands, and use ferries and domestic flights to get around.

Weather: Be aware of the typhoon season (June to November) and plan your travels accordingly.

Local Cuisine: Try local dishes such as adobo, lechon, and sinigang, and enjoy fresh seafood.

13. Myanmar (Burma)

Myanmar offers a unique and relatively untouched travel experience, with ancient temples, friendly locals, and beautiful landscapes.

13.1 Yangon

Shwedagon Pagoda: Visit the Shwedagon Pagoda, one of the most sacred Buddhist sites in Myanmar.

Sule Pagoda: Explore Sule Pagoda, located in the heart of downtown Yangon.

Bogyoke Aung San Market: Shop for handicrafts, jewelry, and souvenirs at Bogyoke Aung San Market.

13.2 Bagan

Temples of Bagan: Explore the thousands of ancient temples and pagodas scattered across the Bagan plains.

Hot Air Balloon Ride: Take a hot air balloon ride over Bagan for a breathtaking view of the temples at sunrise or sunset.

Mount Popa: Visit Mount Popa, an extinct volcano and pilgrimage site with a monastery perched on top.

13.3 Mandalay

Mandalay Hill: Climb Mandalay Hill for panoramic views of the city and surrounding countryside.

Mandalay Palace: Visit the Mandalay Palace, the last royal palace of the Burmese monarchy.

U Bein Bridge: Walk across U Bein Bridge, the world's longest teak bridge, especially beautiful at sunset.

13.4 Inle Lake

Floating Villages: Explore the floating villages and gardens of Inle Lake by boat.

Phaung Daw Oo Pagoda: Visit Phaung Daw Oo Pagoda, an important religious site on the lake.

Nga Hpe Kyaung Monastery: See the unique "jumping cats" at Nga Hpe Kyaung Monastery.

13.5 Ngapali Beach

Beach Relaxation: Relax on the pristine sands of Ngapali Beach, known for its clear waters and laid-back atmosphere.

Fishing Villages: Visit local fishing villages to see traditional fishing methods and experience local life.

13.6 Tips for Traveling in Myanmar

Visa Requirements: Ensure you have the necessary visa and permits for travel in Myanmar.

Currency: Use Myanmar Kyat (MMK) for transactions, and carry cash as credit cards are not widely accepted.

Respect Local Customs: Dress modestly and be respectful when visiting religious sites, and be mindful of cultural norms.

14. Laos

Laos is known for its serene landscapes, friendly people, and rich cultural heritage.

14.1 Luang Prabang

Mount Phousi: Climb Mount Phousi for panoramic views of Luang Prabang and the surrounding mountains.

Kuang Si Falls: Visit Kuang Si Falls, a stunning multi-tiered waterfall with turquoise pools.

Alms Giving Ceremony: Witness the daily alms giving ceremony, where monks collect alms from locals and visitors.

14.2 Vientiane

Pha That Luang: Visit Pha That Luang, the national symbol and most important Buddhist monument in Laos.

Patuxai (Victory Gate): Explore Patuxai, a war monument in the center of Vientiane, reminiscent of the Arc de Triomphe.

Buddha Park: Visit Buddha Park, a unique sculpture park with over 200 Hindu and Buddhist statues.

14.3 Vang Vieng

Tubing on the Nam Song River: Float down the Nam Song River on an inner tube, a popular activity in Vang Vieng.

Tham Chang Cave: Explore Tham Chang Cave, known for its impressive stalactites and stalagmites.

Hot Air Balloon Ride: Take a hot air balloon ride for stunning views of Vang Vieng's karst landscape.

14.4 Plain of Jars

Megalithic Jars: Visit the Plain of Jars, an archaeological site with thousands of large stone jars scattered across the landscape.

Phonsavan: Explore the town of Phonsavan, the gateway to the Plain of Jars, and learn about its history during the Vietnam War.

14.5 Si Phan Don (Four Thousand Islands)

Relaxation: Relax on the islands of Don Det and Don Khon, known for their laid-back atmosphere and beautiful scenery.

Mekong Dolphins: Take a boat trip to see the endangered Irrawaddy dolphins in the Mekong River.

Khone Phapheng Falls: Visit Khone Phapheng Falls, the largest waterfall in Southeast Asia.

14.6 Tips for Traveling in Laos

Transport: Use buses and boats for travel between cities and islands, and consider renting a bicycle or scooter for local exploration.

Currency: Use Lao Kip (LAK) for transactions, and carry cash as credit cards are not widely accepted.

Respect Local Customs: Dress modestly, especially when visiting temples, and be respectful of local customs and traditions.

15. Singapore

Singapore is a modern city-state known for its cleanliness, efficiency, and diverse cultural attractions.

15.1 Marina Bay

Marina Bay Sands: Visit Marina Bay Sands, an iconic hotel with a rooftop infinity pool and observation deck.

Gardens by the Bay: Explore Gardens by the Bay, a futuristic park with Supertree Grove and the Cloud Forest Dome.

Merlion Park: Take a photo with the Merlion, Singapore's famous half-lion, half-fish statue.

15.2 Chinatown

Buddha Tooth Relic Temple: Visit the Buddha Tooth Relic Temple, a stunning Buddhist temple in the heart of Chinatown.

Chinatown Heritage Centre: Learn about the history and culture of Chinatown at the Chinatown Heritage Centre.

Street Food: Sample delicious street food at Chinatown's hawker centers.

15.3 Little India

Sri Veeramakaliamman Temple: Visit Sri Veeramakaliamman Temple, a colorful Hindu temple dedicated to the goddess Kali.

Tekka Centre: Shop for textiles, spices, and food at Tekka Centre, a bustling market in Little India.

Street Art: Explore the vibrant street art and murals in Little India.

15.4 Sentosa Island

Universal Studios Singapore: Spend a day at Universal Studios Singapore, a popular theme park with rides and attractions.

S.E.A. Aquarium: Visit the S.E.A. Aquarium, one of the largest aquariums in the world.

Beaches: Relax on the sandy beaches of Sentosa Island, such as Siloso Beach and Palawan Beach.

15.5 Orchard Road

Shopping: Shop till you drop on Orchard Road, Singapore's premier shopping district with malls, boutiques, and department stores.

ION Orchard: Visit ION Orchard, a luxury shopping mall with a rooftop observation deck.

15.6 Tips for Traveling in Singapore

Public Transport: Use the efficient MRT (Mass Rapid Transit) system to get around the city.

Cleanliness: Follow the strict cleanliness rules, such as no littering or chewing gum in public places.

Respect Local Laws: Be aware of and respect local laws and regulations, including the ban on smoking in certain areas.

Conclusion

Asia offers a wealth of incredible destinations for your gap year, each with its own unique attractions, cultures, and experiences.

Whether you're seeking adventure, cultural immersion, personal growth, or relaxation, there's something for everyone on this diverse continent.

That's what's so amazing about Asia, there's quite literally something for everyone. Whether you're a townie or you love the countryside, or you're a proper beach bum, you'll absolutely love travelling around this continent!

TRAVEL LOGISTICS

Booking Flights and Accommodation

One of the most critical aspects of planning your gap year is ensuring you have reliable and affordable transportation and accommodation. Here's how to navigate the complexities:

Finding the Best Flight Deals

Flexible Dates and Destinations: Use flight comparison websites like Skyscanner, Kayak, or Google Flights to find the best deals. Being flexible with your dates and airports can lead to significant savings.

Booking in Advance: Generally, the earlier you book, the cheaper the flights. Aim to book international flights at least three to six months in advance.

Travel Agencies and Student Discounts: Consider using travel agencies specialising in student or gap year travel. Organizations like STA Travel or Student Universe offer discounts and flexible ticket options.

Layovers and Budget Airlines: Don't shy away from flights with layovers or budget airlines, as they can be more cost-effective. Just ensure you understand their baggage policies to avoid extra fees.

Accommodation Options

Hostels and Budget Hotels: Ideal for gap year travelers on a budget. Websites like Hostelworld and Booking.com are great for finding affordable places to stay.

Airbnb and Vacation Rentals: For longer stays, renting an apartment or house can be more economical and comfortable. Look for options with kitchens to save on food costs.

Volunteering and Work Exchanges: Programs like WWOOF, Workaway, and HelpX offer free accommodation in exchange for volunteer work, which is a great way to immerse yourself in the local culture.

University Dorms and Homestays: In some countries, university dorms are available for rent during the summer, and homestays can provide a more authentic cultural experience.

Packing Essentials

Packing for a gap year requires careful consideration to ensure you have everything you need without overloading yourself.

Essential Items

Documents: Passport, visas, travel insurance, copies of important documents, and any required vaccination certificates.

Clothing: Pack versatile, weather-appropriate clothing that can be layered. Remember essentials like a waterproof jacket, comfortable walking shoes, and a few sets of quick-dry clothing.

Electronics: A smartphone with a local SIM card, a laptop or tablet, and necessary chargers and adapters. Consider a portable power bank for long travel days.

First Aid Kit: Include basic medical supplies such as band-aids, antiseptic wipes, pain relievers, any prescription medications, and travel sickness tablets.

Toiletries: Travel-sized toiletries to save space, and any specific items you might not find abroad.

Travel Gear

Backpack or Suitcase?

That is the eternal debate.

Choose based on your travel style. A sturdy, comfortable backpack is ideal for those constantly on the move, while a suitcase might be better for longer stays in one place.

Bear in mind that no one wants to be that person who's dragging their suitcase from a Thai boat up to the beach, getting all their stuff soaked in the process, so think carefully about where you might go before you choose your luggage.

I have a fantastic, sturdy Osprey rucksack that has been ideal for many excursions, but I also have a smaller rucksack for trips that are more appropriate, so pick wisely (and know that you can always swap out and buy another style of luggage abroad if you need to, depending on where you go).

Of course, I have also nearly broken my back SO MANY TIMES from carting around a huge rucksack full of stuff I didn't need, so picking your bag also depends on what you're planning to bring. I started out with a snorkel and a hairdryer (and a she-wee that my mum bought me) and abandoned all three in hostels fairly quickly.

It's also become fairly 'cool' to have a smaller rucksack, and I got a few comments from cool people in hostels who were travelling with one small bag filled with a swimsuit and a pack of noodles. I cannot travel that light, fact, but if you do want to just have a teeny bag, know that you're not alone.

Daypack: A smaller backpack for daily excursions and short trips. Really recommend bringing one of these, as sometimes you might want to leave your big bag somewhere while you embark on a one- or two-day adventure.

Packing Cubes: To organise your clothing and gear efficiently. I always start out with the best intentions, putting everything in packing cubes, and end up chucking everything haphazardly into my bag by the end, but you might be more organised!

Managing Travel Documents

Having the right documents and managing them properly is crucial for smooth travels.

Passports and Visas

Passports: Ensure your passport is valid for at least six months beyond your planned return date. Keep digital and physical copies.

Visas: Research visa requirements for each country you plan to visit. Some countries offer visa-on-arrival, while others require advance applications. Websites like iVisa or the government's official sites can provide up-to-date information.

Travel Insurance

Comprehensive Coverage: Choose travel insurance that covers medical emergencies, trip cancellations, theft, and natural disasters. Providers like World Nomads and SafetyWing specialize in travel insurance for long-term travelers.

Emergency Contacts: Keep a list of emergency contacts, including your insurance company, local embassies, and family members.

Money Management

Managing your finances while traveling is crucial to ensure you don't run out of money unexpectedly.

Banking and Currency

Bank Accounts: Consider opening an international bank account or one with low foreign transaction fees. Notify your bank of your travel plans to avoid any issues.

Local Currency: Carry a mix of local currency and a debit/credit card. Use ATMs to withdraw cash but be mindful of fees.

Try not to carry too much cash, as this can make you a target for pickpockets, but also try and have around £100/ $100 handy just in case (assuming you have at least one bank card, ideally a few, that work abroad. I have known people to only carry one card and then face issues when this card has stopped working - I really would recommending having more than one debit card with you when you travel.

Alternatively, I was given this advice - "As long as you have your passport and credit card on you, you can always get home" - before I set off, and so having a good credit card as a back-up is wise.

Budgeting Tools

At the end of this chapter, I'll give an idea of the sort of budget you might need for your travels.

However, expense Tracking Apps: Apps like Trail Wallet, Trabee Pocket, or Mint can help you keep track of your spending and stay within budget.

Cash and Emergency Funds: Always have a small amount of emergency cash hidden in a secure place, separate from your main wallet.

Staying Connected

Maintaining communication with family and friends is essential for safety and peace of mind.

Mobile Phones and SIM Cards

Unlocked Phones: Ensure your phone is unlocked so you can use local SIM cards, which are often the cheapest way to stay connected.

International Plans: Alternatively, look into international plans offered by your carrier.

Internet Access

Wi-Fi: Many hostels, cafes, and public places offer free Wi-Fi. Apps like WiFi Map can help you find nearby hotspots.

Portable Hotspots: For consistent internet access, consider renting or buying a portable Wi-Fi device.

Emergency Preparedness

Being prepared for emergencies can make a significant difference in crisis situations.

Emergency Contacts and Plans

Local Contacts: Have a list of local emergency numbers, including police, medical services, and your country's embassy or consulate.

Emergency Plans: Develop a basic emergency plan, including evacuation routes and meeting points.

Health and Safety Kits

First Aid Kit: As mentioned, always have a basic first aid kit.

Safety Gear: Depending on your activities, safety gear like a whistle, personal alarm, or multi-tool can be useful.

By mastering the logistics of travel, you'll ensure a smoother, more enjoyable gap year experience. The next chapters will delve into living abroad, finding work and volunteer opportunities, and making the most of your time away from home.

HOW MUCH DOES A GAP YEAR COST?

How long is a piece of string?

No, I'm joking. It's incredibly hard to estimate your total, because everyone has different things that they want to do - if you want to go ski-ing in Canada for a month, you're going to spend a helluva lot more than someone who wants to live the hostel life in Java.

However, I can give an idea of averages, and the type of things you need to budget for. Please note that I'll put all my costs in dollars (as I do on my YouTube channel, @nomadvieve), because this is a commonly known currency (in fact, you'll be surprised how many countries actually take dollars as payment! When I went, I took $200 along with me, as they're easier to change (if needed) than British Pounds, and I spent it without having to change it into any local currency).

A gap year can vary widely in cost depending on your destination, activities, and lifestyle. Understanding the various expenses involved can help you plan and budget effectively.

Major Cost Categories

Travel: Flights, transportation, and travel insurance.
Accommodation: Hostels, hotels, rentals, and homestays.
Food and Daily Living: Meals, groceries, and daily necessities.

Activities and Experiences: Tours, excursions, and cultural experiences.

Health and Safety: Vaccinations, medical supplies, and insurance.

Miscellaneous: Visas, permits, and unexpected expenses.

Transportation Costs

Transportation is a significant expense in a gap year budget, encompassing both international and local travel.

International Flights

Round-Trip Tickets: Costs can vary greatly depending on your destination and the time of year. On average, international round-trip flights can range from $500 to $1,500.

Booking Tips: Book flights well in advance, use comparison websites like Skyscanner, and look for student discounts.

Local Transportation

Public Transport: Buses, trains, and subways are usually the most cost-effective options. Monthly passes can save money, averaging $30 to $100 per month depending on the city.

Taxis and Ride-Sharing: Use these options sparingly as they can add up quickly. Budget $50 to $100 per month if needed.

Car Rentals and Bikes: In some regions, renting a car or bike may be necessary. Car rentals can range from $20 to $50 per day, while bike rentals are typically $10 to $20 per day.

Accommodation Costs

Accommodation will likely be one of your largest expenses, but it varies widely based on location and type.

Hostels and Budget Hotels

Hostels: Dormitory beds in hostels typically cost $10 to $30 per night, making them a budget-friendly option.

Budget Hotels: Expect to pay $30 to $60 per night for basic hotel rooms.

Long-Term Rentals and Homestays

Renting Apartments: Monthly rents can vary greatly. In major cities, expect to pay $500 to $1,500 per month for a modest apartment.

Homestays: These can be more affordable and offer cultural immersion. Costs range from $300 to $800 per month, often including some meals.

Food and Daily Living Expenses

Daily living expenses, particularly food, are essential to budget carefully.

Eating Out

Local Restaurants: Eating at local eateries and street food stalls is cheaper, averaging $3 to $10 per meal.

Western Restaurants: Meals at more upscale or Western restaurants can cost $10 to $30 each.

Groceries and Cooking

Grocery Costs: Cooking for yourself can save money. Monthly grocery bills can range from $100 to $300, depending on the country.

Markets: Buying fresh produce from local markets can be more affordable and a great way to experience local culture.

Activity and Experience Costs

Engaging in activities and experiences is a key part of a gap year, but these can add up.

Tours and Excursions

Guided Tours: Prices vary widely. Local tours can be as low as $20, while multi-day guided tours may range from $100 to $1,000.

Self-Guided Experiences: These can be more affordable, requiring only entrance fees and transportation costs.

Cultural and Leisure Activities

Museums and Attractions: Entrance fees can range from $5 to $25 per visit.

Outdoor Activities: Costs for hiking, diving, or adventure sports vary. Budget $50 to $200 per activity.

Health and Safety Costs

Ensuring your health and safety is essential and comes with its own set of costs.

Vaccinations and Medical Supplies

Vaccinations: Depending on your destination, vaccinations can cost $100 to $500.

Medical Supplies: A basic first aid kit and any personal medications should be budgeted at $50 to $100.

Travel Insurance

Comprehensive Coverage: Travel insurance that covers medical emergencies, trip cancellations, and theft can cost $30 to $100 per month.

Miscellaneous Costs

Miscellaneous costs can include visas, permits, and unexpected expenses.

Visas and Permits

Visa Fees: Visa fees vary by country, typically ranging from $30 to $200 per visa.

Permit Costs: Some countries require permits for work or extended stays, which can add additional costs.

Unexpected Expenses

Contingency Fund: Budget an extra $500 to $1,000 for unexpected expenses such as emergency travel, gear replacement, or medical issues.

Budgeting and Saving Tips

Effective budgeting and saving strategies can help manage your gap year expenses.

Creating a Budget

Monthly Budget: Track your monthly expenses and income using apps like Mint or YNAB.

Adjust as Needed: Be flexible and adjust your budget based on actual spending.

Saving Money

Work and Volunteer: Look for work or volunteer opportunities that offer free accommodation and meals.

Discount Cards: Use student or youth discount cards for travel, accommodation, and activities.

Financial Safety Nets

Emergency Fund: Keep an emergency fund separate from your main travel funds.

Banking: Use a bank with low foreign transaction fees and ensure you have access to funds in case of emergencies.

Sample Budget Breakdown

Here's a sample monthly budget for a gap year traveler in a moderately priced country:

Accommodation: $500 (rented apartment)
Food: $250 (groceries and occasional eating out)
Local Transportation: $50 (public transport pass)
Activities and Experiences: $200 (tours, museum entries, etc.)
Travel Insurance: $50
Miscellaneous: $100 (visas, unexpected expenses)
Total Monthly Budget: $1,150

Final Thoughts on Gap Year Costs

While the cost of a gap year can be substantial, careful planning and budgeting can make it more manageable. By understanding the different expenses and finding ways to save, you can make the most of your gap year without breaking the bank. The experiences and personal growth you gain will be invaluable, making the investment worthwhile.

LIVING ABROAD

Adapting to New Cultures

Living abroad is a transformative experience that requires adaptability and openness to new ways of life. Here's how to navigate cultural differences and make the most of your time in a foreign country:

<u>Understanding Cultural Norms</u>

Research and Respect: Before arriving, research the local customs, traditions, and social norms of your destination. Show respect by adhering to these practices.

Observe and Ask: Observe the behavior of locals and ask questions if you're unsure about something. Most people are happy to explain their culture to respectful newcomers.

<u>Managing Culture Shock</u>

Initial Reactions: It's normal to experience culture shock, which can manifest as homesickness, frustration, or anxiety. Acknowledge these feelings as part of the adjustment process.

Stay Positive: Focus on the positive aspects of your new environment. Embrace the differences and try to learn from them. Don't ignore the bad feelings, but also try and practise gratitude where you can.

Create a Routine: Establishing a daily routine can provide a sense of normalcy and help you adjust more quickly. Having a routine that you can get into before you go - for example, spraying pillow spray every night before you go to sleep - can help you when you're away, by tricking your brain into thinking that it's just another normal night.

Building Cultural Sensitivity

Be Open-Minded: Approach new experiences with an open mind. Avoid making quick judgments based on your own cultural standards.

Language Learning: Even a basic understanding of the local language can go a long way in building connections and showing respect. Google Translate can be a saviour.

Finding Accommodation

Securing safe and comfortable accommodation is essential for a successful stay abroad. Here are some options and tips for finding the right place to live:

Types of Accommodation

Hostels: Ideal for short-term stays and meeting other travelers. Hostels are affordable and often located in central areas.

Apartments: Renting an apartment is suitable for longer stays and provides more privacy. Websites like Airbnb, Booking.com, and local real estate agencies can help you find listings.

Homestays: Living with a local family offers cultural immersion and can be a cost-effective option. It's also a great way to improve your language skills.

University Dorms: Some universities rent out dorm rooms to travelers during the summer. This can be a budget-friendly and social option.

Tips for Securing Accommodation

Research Thoroughly: Read reviews and check ratings on accommodation websites to ensure the place is reputable and safe.

Book in Advance: Secure your first few nights of accommodation before you arrive. This gives you a base while you search for longer-term options.

Visit in Person: If possible, visit the accommodation in person before committing to a long-term lease to ensure it meets your expectations.

Navigating Transportation

Getting around in a new country can be challenging but understanding the local transportation system is crucial for exploring and commuting.

Public Transportation

Buses and Trains: Most cities have reliable bus and train systems. Learn the routes, schedules, and ticketing options. Apps like Google Maps and local transit apps can help. Carry small notes in cash, in case they don't take card. Check out apps in advance - for example, in Thailand and Bali, the Grab app saved me every time I needed a taxi.

Subways and Trams: In many large cities, subways and trams are the quickest way to get around. Familiarise yourself with the lines and stations.

Alternative Transportation

Bicycles: In many cities, cycling is a popular and eco-friendly way to travel. Look for bike rental services or consider buying a second-hand bike if you're there for a while. Hoi An is a fantastic place to cycle around, if you visit Vietnam.

Ride-Sharing and Taxis: Services like Uber, Lyft, and local taxi apps provide convenient options for getting around, especially late at night or in areas with limited public transport.

Renting a Vehicle

Cars and Scooters: If you plan to travel outside of cities, renting a car or scooter might be necessary. Make sure you have an international driver's license and understand the local traffic laws.

Car-Sharing Services: Companies like Zipcar and local equivalents offer car-sharing options for short-term rentals.

Integrating into the Community

Building a social network and integrating into the local community will enhance your experience and help you feel more at home.

Making Friends

Join Groups and Clubs: Look for local clubs, sports teams, or interest groups to meet people with similar interests. Facebook can be a great tool for finding out what's on, as well as looking at events run by your hostel.

Attend Events: Participate in local events, festivals, and community gatherings. Websites like Meetup can help you find social events.

Volunteering and Work

Volunteer Opportunities: Volunteering is a great way to give back to the community and meet new people. Organizations like WWOOF and local charities often seek volunteers.

Part-Time Jobs: Working part-time can provide financial support and help you integrate into the local culture. Research visa regulations to ensure you're allowed to work.

Language Exchange

Language Classes: Enroll in local language classes to improve your communication skills and meet other learners.

Language Exchange Partners: Find language exchange partners through local universities, community centers, or online platforms.

Staying Healthy and Safe

Maintaining your health and safety is paramount while living abroad. Here are some tips to ensure you stay well and secure.

Health Care

Local Health Services: Familiarize yourself with the local healthcare system. Know where the nearest hospitals and clinics are located.

Health Insurance: Ensure your travel insurance covers medical expenses. Consider purchasing additional health insurance if necessary.

Healthy Habits: Maintain a balanced diet, exercise regularly, and get enough sleep to keep your immune system strong.

<u>Personal Safety</u>

Stay Informed: Keep up to date with local news and be aware of any safety advisories or travel warnings.

Emergency Contacts: Have a list of emergency contacts, including local authorities, your country's embassy, and close family or friends.

Street Smarts: Be mindful of your surroundings, especially in unfamiliar or crowded areas. Avoid displaying valuables and use caution when withdrawing cash or using ATMs.

Legal Considerations

Understanding the legal landscape of your host country is crucial for avoiding any potential issues.

<u>Visa and Immigration</u>

Visa Requirements: Ensure you have the correct visa for your stay and understand the conditions attached

to it. Regularly check the expiry dates and renewal processes.
Residency Permits: Some countries require long-term visitors to obtain residency permits. Research the requirements and process for your destination.

Local Laws

Know the Rules: Familiarize yourself with local laws and regulations, including those related to alcohol, drugs, and public behaviour.

Stay Compliant: Always carry a copy of your identification and visa documents. Adhere to local laws and respect law enforcement officials.

By understanding and preparing for these aspects of living abroad, you can ensure a smoother, more enjoyable experience. The next chapters will explore opportunities for volunteering and working, staying connected, and maximising your gap year adventures.

HOSTEL LIFE

Staying in hostels is a popular choice for travelers, especially those on a gap year. Hostels offer affordable accommodation, a chance to meet fellow travelers, and often a unique and social atmosphere.

This chapter will guide you through everything you need to know about staying in hostels, from booking and packing to making the most of your stay and ensuring your safety.

1. Choosing the Right Hostel

1.1 Research and Reviews

Read Reviews: Use websites like Hostelworld, HostelBookers, and TripAdvisor to read reviews and ratings from other travelers. Look for feedback on cleanliness, security, location, and atmosphere.

Check Photos: Review photos of the hostel to get a sense of the facilities and overall vibe. Look for images of common areas, dorm rooms, bathrooms, and any unique features.

1.2 Location

Proximity to Attractions: Choose a hostel that is conveniently located near the main attractions or activities you want to explore.

Public Transport: Ensure the hostel is close to public transport options like buses, trains, or metro stations.

Safety: Research the safety of the neighborhood, especially if you plan to return late at night.

1.3 Facilities and Amenities

Common Areas: Look for hostels with comfortable common areas where you can relax and socialize.

Kitchen Facilities: A well-equipped kitchen allows you to save money by cooking your own meals.

Wi-Fi and Internet: Free Wi-Fi is essential for staying connected and planning your travels.

Laundry Facilities: Having access to laundry facilities can be convenient for long-term travelers.

Lockers and Security: Ensure the hostel provides lockers to secure your valuables.

1.4 Atmosphere

Social vs. Quiet: Decide whether you want a lively, social atmosphere or a quieter, more relaxed environment.
Party hostels are great for meeting people and having fun, while quieter hostels are better for rest and relaxation.

Events and Activities: Some hostels organize events like pub crawls, tours, and game nights, which can be a great way to meet other travelers.

2. Booking Your Stay

2.1 Booking Platforms

Hostelworld and HostelBookers: These platforms offer a wide selection of hostels worldwide and allow you to compare prices, read reviews, and book directly.

Booking.com: This site also features many hostels and often has flexible cancellation policies.

Direct Booking: Some hostels offer better rates or special deals if you book directly through their website.

2.2 Timing and Availability

Advance Booking: Book in advance during peak travel seasons or popular events to ensure availability and secure the best rates.

Flexible Booking: If your travel plans are flexible, consider booking a few days at a time. This allows you to change hostels if you don't like the first one or extend your stay if you do.

2.3 Payment and Cancellation Policies

Deposit Requirements: Some hostels require a deposit at the time of booking. Check the policies and be prepared to pay this upfront.

Cancellation Policy: Familiarize yourself with the hostel's cancellation policy in case your plans change. Look for options with free cancellation if your itinerary is uncertain.

3. Packing for Your Hostel Stay

3.1 Essentials

Lock: Bring a sturdy padlock for securing your belongings in lockers.

Towel: Many hostels do not provide towels, so pack a quick-dry travel towel.

Toiletries: Bring your own toiletries, including shampoo, soap, toothpaste, and a toothbrush.

Flip-Flops: Pack a pair of flip-flops for the showers and walking around the hostel.

3.2 Comfortable Clothing

Loungewear: Bring comfortable clothes for lounging around the hostel.

Sleepwear: Pack appropriate sleepwear for shared dorm rooms.

Layers: Hostels can vary in temperature, so bring layers to stay comfortable.

3.3 Bedding

Sleep Sack or Sheet: Some budget hostels charge for linens or have questionable cleanliness. A lightweight sleep sack or travel sheet can be a good backup.

Earplugs and Eye Mask: Dorm rooms can be noisy and bright. Earplugs and an eye mask can help you sleep better.

3.4 Electronics and Gadgets

Power Adapter: Bring a universal power adapter to charge your devices.

Portable Charger: A portable power bank can be useful for keeping your devices charged on the go.

Headphones: Noise-canceling headphones or earbuds are great for blocking out noise and listening to music or podcasts.

4. Making the Most of Your Hostel Stay

4.1 Socializing

Introduce Yourself: Be open and introduce yourself to fellow travelers. A simple "Hi, where are you from?" can start a great conversation.

Join Activities: Participate in hostel-organized activities and events. These are designed to help guests meet and socialize.

Common Areas: Spend time in common areas like lounges, kitchens, and rooftop terraces to meet other travelers.

4.2 Cooking and Eating

Shared Meals: Cook shared meals with other guests. It's a fun way to bond and share culinary skills.

Local Markets: Shop at local markets for fresh ingredients and try cooking local dishes.

Food Storage: Label your food and store it in designated areas in the hostel kitchen to avoid confusion and ensure it stays safe.

4.3 Staying Organized

Keep Your Space Tidy: Respect your dorm mates by keeping your belongings organized and your area clean.

Pack Efficiently: Use packing cubes or compression bags to keep your luggage organized and easily accessible.

Laundry: Take advantage of laundry facilities to keep your clothes clean. Don't leave your laundry unattended for long periods.

4.4 Safety and Security

Use Lockers: Always store your valuables in lockers provided by the hostel. Use your own padlock for added security.

Be Aware: Stay aware of your surroundings and the people you meet. Trust your instincts and avoid sharing too much personal information.

Travel Insurance: Ensure you have travel insurance that covers theft and loss of belongings.

5. Hostel Etiquette

5.1 Respecting Dorm Mates

Noise Levels: Keep noise to a minimum, especially late at night and early in the morning. Use headphones for listening to music or watching videos.

Lights: Use a flashlight or your phone's light if you need to find something in the dark. Avoid turning on the main light in the dorm room.

Cleanliness: Keep your area clean and tidy. Don't leave personal items scattered around the room or bathroom.

5.2 Shared Spaces

Kitchen Etiquette: Clean up after yourself in the kitchen. Wash your dishes, wipe down surfaces, and put away any shared items.

Bathrooms: Leave the bathroom clean and tidy for the next person. Don't hog the facilities, especially during peak times.

Common Areas: Be mindful of others in common areas. Share seating and facilities, and avoid monopolizing space or resources.

5.3 Cultural Sensitivity

Cultural Differences: Be aware of and respect cultural differences among fellow travelers. What's acceptable in one culture may not be in another.

Language: Try to use a common language when in group settings to include everyone in the conversation.

Personal Space: Respect personal space and boundaries. Not everyone is comfortable with physical touch or close proximity.

6. Long-Term Hostel Stays

6.1 Choosing a Suitable Hostel

Monthly Rates: Look for hostels that offer discounted rates for long-term stays.

Facilities: Ensure the hostel has the necessary facilities for a comfortable long-term stay, such as a kitchen, laundry, and reliable Wi-Fi.

Community: Consider the atmosphere and community vibe. A hostel with a supportive and friendly community can make a long-term stay more enjoyable.

6.2 Managing Belongings

Storage Solutions: Use packing cubes, organizers, and storage bins to keep your belongings tidy and easily accessible.

Space-Saving Hacks: Implement space-saving hacks, such as rolling clothes and using multi-purpose items, to maximize your living area.

6.3 Building a Routine

Daily Routine: Establish a daily routine that includes work, exercise, meals, and relaxation. This can help you maintain a sense of normalcy and productivity.

Social Connections: Build strong social connections with other long-term guests. Participate in hostel activities and organize group outings.

7. Handling Common Issues

7.1 Noise and Sleep Disruptions

Earplugs and White Noise: Use earplugs or a white noise app to block out noise and ensure a better night's sleep.

Communication: Politely communicate with noisy dorm mates. Most travelers are considerate and will quiet down if asked respectfully.

7.2 Cleanliness and Hygiene

Self-Cleaning: Take initiative to clean up after yourself and encourage others to do the same.

Reporting Issues: Report any cleanliness or hygiene issues to hostel staff. They can address the problem and ensure a clean environment for everyone.

7.3 Safety Concerns

Trust Your Instincts: If you feel unsafe, trust your instincts and take action. This could mean moving to a different hostel or reporting concerns to staff.

Stay Informed: Stay informed about local safety advisories and follow any guidelines provided by the hostel.

8. Conclusion

Staying in hostels can be one of the most rewarding aspects of your gap year, offering opportunities to meet new people, save money, and immerse yourself in different cultures.

By choosing the right hostel, packing smartly, making the most of your stay, respecting hostel etiquette, and handling common issues effectively, you can ensure a safe, comfortable, and enjoyable hostel experience.

Embrace the social nature of hostels, and you'll likely make lifelong friends and unforgettable memories.

VOLUNTEERING AND WORK OPPORTUNITIES

Volunteering Abroad

Volunteering during your gap year can be a rewarding way to give back to communities, gain new skills, and immerse yourself in different cultures. Here's how to find and make the most of volunteer opportunities abroad:

Finding Reputable Programs

Research Organizations: Look for well-established, reputable organizations with positive reviews and clear, transparent operations. Websites like Volunteer World, GoAbroad, and Idealist can help you find programs.

Understand the Commitment: Make sure you understand the time commitment and responsibilities involved. Some programs require a minimum stay, while others are more flexible.

Check for Hidden Costs: Some volunteer programs charge fees to cover accommodation, food, and other expenses. Ensure you know what's included and budget accordingly.

Types of Volunteer Work

Community Development: Work on projects that improve local infrastructure, education, and healthcare. This might include building schools, teaching, or working in clinics.

Side note: I had a friend who went to Cambodia to help paint a mural on the side of a school. Her and her group paid to do this, and spent a gruelling week painting the whole mural. She went back a few weeks later and they'd painted over it, ready for the next batch of tourists to paint it again. This isn't necessarily an issue - after all, they needed the money and they still recieved it - but check out reviews for the programme you're looking at, so that you're making the type of impact that you want to make.

Environmental Conservation: Participate in projects that protect wildlife and the environment. This could involve working in national parks, conducting wildlife research, or participating in reforestation efforts.

Education and Teaching: Teach English or other subjects in schools, community centers, or as part of after-school programs. TEFL (Teaching English as a

Foreign Language) certification can be helpful but is not always required.

Making a Positive Impact

Cultural Sensitivity: Approach your volunteer work with respect and openness. Understand that you are there to support the community, not impose your own ideas.

Sustainable Contributions: Focus on projects that have long-term benefits for the community. Avoid programs that might create dependency rather than empowering local people.

Reflect and Learn: Regularly reflect on your experiences, learn from them, and adapt as needed. Your goal should be to leave a positive, lasting impact.

Working While Traveling

Finding work during your gap year can help fund your travels and provide valuable professional experience. Here's how to navigate the job market abroad:

Types of Jobs for Travelers

Hospitality and Tourism: Jobs in hotels, hostels, restaurants, and tour companies are often available to travelers. These positions can include front desk work, housekeeping, bartending, or tour guiding.

Teaching English: As mentioned earlier, teaching English is a popular option. Many countries have high demand for English teachers, and positions can range from formal school settings to private tutoring.

Seasonal Work: Depending on the season, you might find work in agriculture (e.g., fruit picking), ski resorts, or summer camps. These jobs are often temporary and cater to the influx of tourists during peak seasons.

Side note: I had a friend who ran out of money while on Koh Rong, the Cambodian island (highly recommended, by the way - it's beautiful and the Mad Monkey hostel there is a lot of fun). Instead of panicking and asking her parents to fly her home, she was able to get a job in a bar for a few weeks, which allowed her to save up enough to carry on to her next destination. Sometimes, it's worth asking around.

Finding Work Abroad

Job Boards and Websites: Websites like Workaway, WWOOF, and HelpX connect travelers with work opportunities. Additionally, platforms like LinkedIn, Indeed, and local job boards can be useful.

Networking: Connect with other travelers, expats, and locals. Word of mouth can often lead to job opportunities that aren't advertised online.

Work Visas: Research the visa requirements for working in your destination country. Some countries offer working holiday visas specifically for travelers.

Balancing Work and Travel

Part-Time and Flexible Jobs: Look for jobs that offer flexible hours or part-time schedules, allowing you to explore and travel during your free time.

Budgeting and Saving: Use your earnings to cover travel expenses and save for future adventures. Create a budget to manage your income and expenses effectively.

Internships and Skill Development

Internships provide a unique opportunity to gain professional experience and develop skills relevant to your future career.

Finding Internships Abroad

University Programs: Many universities have partnerships with organizations abroad and offer internship placements for students and alumni.

Internship Placement Services: Companies like Intern Abroad HQ and Global Experiences specialize in placing interns in international positions.

Direct Applications: Reach out to companies and organizations directly. Tailor your resume and cover letter to highlight your skills and enthusiasm for the position.

Maximizing Your Internship Experience

Set Clear Goals: Before starting, define what you hope to achieve from your internship. This could include specific skills you want to develop, projects you want to work on, or professional contacts you aim to make.

Be Proactive: Take initiative, seek out learning opportunities, and show enthusiasm for your work. Don't be afraid to ask questions and seek feedback.

Build Your Network: Establish connections with colleagues and professionals in your field. Networking can open doors to future job opportunities and provide valuable references.

Combining Volunteering, Work, and Travel

Many gap year travelers choose to combine volunteering, work, and travel to maximize their experiences and make the most of their time abroad.

Creating a Balanced Itinerary

Mixing Activities: Plan a mix of volunteering, work, and travel to keep your itinerary varied and exciting.

For example, you might spend a few months working in one country, followed by a volunteering stint in another, and then travel for leisure.

Time Management: Allocate time for rest and exploration between work and volunteering commitments. This balance will help prevent burnout and allow you to enjoy your travels fully.

Financial Planning

Income and Expenses: Use the income from work to fund your travels and cover living expenses. Volunteering can often provide free accommodation and meals, helping you save money.

Emergency Fund: Keep an emergency fund for unexpected expenses or emergencies. This financial cushion can give you peace of mind while traveling.

Personal and Professional Growth

Both volunteering and working abroad offer significant opportunities for personal and professional growth.

Developing Soft Skills

Communication: Interacting with people from different cultures enhances your communication skills and cultural sensitivity.

Adaptability: Navigating new environments and overcoming challenges builds resilience and adaptability.

Problem-Solving: Working in diverse settings requires creative problem-solving and critical thinking.

Building Your Resume

International Experience: Highlight your international experience on your resume. Employers value candidates who have demonstrated independence, adaptability, and cross-cultural communication.

Skills and Achievements: Document the skills you've developed and the achievements you've made during your gap year. Be prepared to discuss these experiences in job interviews.

Reflecting on Your Experiences

Regular reflection helps you make the most of your gap year experiences and understand their impact on your personal and professional development.

Keeping a Journal

Documenting Experiences: Keep a journal to document your daily experiences, thoughts, and reflections. This record will be valuable for remembering details and reflecting on your growth.

Goal Review: Periodically review your goals and assess your progress. Adjust your plans as needed to ensure you're on track to achieve what you set out to do.

Sharing Your Story

Blogging and Social Media: Share your experiences through a blog or social media platforms. This not only keeps friends and family updated but also helps you connect with other travelers and volunteers.

Presentations and Talks: Consider giving presentations or talks about your gap year experiences. This can be a great way to share what you've learned and inspire others.

By engaging in volunteering and work opportunities, you can make a meaningful impact, gain valuable skills, and enrich your gap year experience. The next chapters will focus on exploring and enjoying your year, staying connected, and documenting your journey.

EXPLORING AND ENJOYING YOUR YEAR

Top Activities and Experiences

Your gap year is a unique opportunity to engage in activities and experiences that will shape your personal growth and create lifelong memories. Here are some must-do activities to consider:

Adventure and Outdoor Activities

Hiking and Trekking: Explore natural landscapes by hiking in national parks, mountain ranges, and scenic trails. Notable treks include the Inca Trail in Peru, the Camino de Santiago in Spain, and the Annapurna Circuit in Nepal.

Water Sports: Try snorkeling, scuba diving, surfing, kayaking, and sailing in various locations. The Great Barrier Reef in Australia, the beaches of Bali, and the fjords of Norway offer excellent water activities.

Extreme Sports: If you're an adrenaline junkie, consider bungee jumping, skydiving, paragliding, and white-water rafting. New Zealand, Switzerland, and Costa Rica are known for their adventure sports.

Cultural Experiences

Local Festivals: Participate in local festivals and celebrations to immerse yourself in the culture. Examples include Carnival in Brazil, Diwali in India, and the Lantern Festival in Taiwan.

Historical Sites: Visit historical landmarks and UNESCO World Heritage sites. Explore ancient ruins, castles, temples, and museums to learn about the history and heritage of each location.

Culinary Adventures: Sample local cuisines and take cooking classes. Food markets, street vendors, and traditional restaurants offer authentic flavors and culinary experiences.

Arts and Entertainment

Performing Arts: Attend local theater performances, music concerts, dance shows, and festivals. Cities like London, New York, and Tokyo offer world-class entertainment.
Art Galleries and Museums: Explore art galleries and museums to appreciate local art and history. Paris, Florence, and Amsterdam are renowned for their art collections.

Traveling Smart

Traveling smartly involves making sustainable, responsible, and well-planned choices. Here's how to be a savvy traveler:

Sustainable Travel

Eco-Friendly Accommodations: Choose eco-friendly hotels, hostels, and lodges that prioritize sustainability and environmental responsibility.

Responsible Tourism: Support local businesses, avoid exploitative activities, and respect wildlife. Opt for ethical tours and experiences that benefit the local community.

Minimise Waste: Reduce plastic use by carrying reusable water bottles, bags, and utensils. Be mindful of your waste and recycle when possible. Some countries (e.g., Thailand) have free water bottle refill schemes, so look this up in advance. Nearly every hostel that I've stayed in will fill your bottle up for free, and so there's usually very little reason to buy single-use plastic bottles on your travels.

Budget Travel Tips

Travel Off-Peak: Avoid peak tourist seasons to save money and enjoy a more authentic experience. Off-peak travel often means lower prices and fewer crowds.

Use Public Transportation: Public transportation is usually cheaper and more environmentally friendly than taxis or rental cars. Learn to navigate buses, trains, and metro systems.

Stay in Hostels and Budget Accommodations: Hostels, guesthouses, and budget hotels offer affordable lodging options. Consider staying in dormitory rooms to save even more.

Safety and Security

Stay Informed: Keep up-to-date with local news and travel advisories. Register with your embassy if available.
Travel Insurance: Always have travel insurance that covers medical emergencies, trip cancellations, and theft. Carry a copy of your insurance details with you.

Be Prepared: Carry a small first aid kit, have emergency contacts handy, and always know the local emergency numbers.

Social Life and Making Friends

Building a social network while traveling enhances your experience and provides support. Here's how to meet people and make friends on your gap year:

Staying in Social Accommodations

Hostels: Hostels are excellent for meeting other travelers. Many hostels organize social events, tours, and activities that make it easy to connect with others.

Homestays: Staying with local families provides cultural immersion and the opportunity to build meaningful relationships.

Joining Groups and Clubs

Local Clubs and Classes: Join local clubs, sports teams, or take classes to meet people with similar interests. Language classes, dance lessons, and cooking workshops are great options.

Expats and Travelers Groups: Look for expat communities and travelers' groups on platforms like Meetup, Facebook, and Couchsurfing.

Participating in Tours and Activities

Group Tours: Joining group tours can be a great way to meet fellow travelers. Whether it's a day tour or a multi-day adventure, shared experiences foster connections.

Volunteer Programs: Volunteering provides a common purpose and often leads to lasting friendships. Working on projects together helps build bonds with other volunteers and locals.

Staying Connected and Documenting Your Journey

Keeping in touch with loved ones and documenting your experiences helps you stay connected and preserve memories.

Communication Tools

Messaging Apps: Use apps like WhatsApp, Skype, and Viber to stay in touch with family and friends. Ensure you have a reliable internet connection. It might be worth setting up a regular call with your family - e.g., every Sunday - so that you have a fixed routine in the diary. The timing can vary depending on where you are, but this enables you to check in (and whether you want or not, having these calls can really help your mental state!)

Social Media: Share updates and photos on social media platforms like Instagram, Facebook, and Twitter. This not only keeps loved ones informed but also helps you connect with fellow travelers.

Blogging and Vlogging

Create a Blog: Start a travel blog to document your experiences, share tips, and keep a record of your journey. Platforms like WordPress and Blogger are user-friendly and popular among travelers.

Vlogging: If you prefer video, consider starting a vlog on YouTube or Vimeo. Vlogging allows you to capture the sights and sounds of your travels, making your memories more vivid.

Keeping a Journal

Daily Entries: Write daily entries in a travel journal to capture your thoughts, experiences, and reflections. This can be a personal keepsake and a source of inspiration for future travels.

Creative Documentation: Use sketches, collages, and other creative methods to document your journey. Collect mementos like tickets, postcards, and brochures to create a scrapbook.

Reflecting and Growing

Regular reflection helps you make the most of your gap year and recognise the growth you've achieved.

Regular Reflection

Weekly Reviews: Set aside time each week to review your experiences, challenges, and achievements. Consider what you've learned and how you've grown.

Goal Assessment: Revisit your goals periodically to assess your progress and make adjustments as needed. This ensures you stay on track and continue to make meaningful progress.

Personal Growth

Embrace Change: Recognise that living abroad and traveling will change you. Embrace the new perspectives and insights you gain, and let them shape your future.

Skill Development: Identify the skills you've developed during your gap year, such as adaptability, problem-solving, and communication. Consider how these skills will benefit you in your personal and professional life.

By exploring and enjoying your gap year to the fullest, you'll create lasting memories, gain valuable experiences, and grow in ways you never imagined. The next chapters will cover staying connected and documenting your journey, as well as health and wellbeing while living abroad.

HOW TO TALK TO ANYONE

Traveling provides countless opportunities to meet new people, make friends, and gain insights into different cultures and perspectives. Mastering the art of conversation can significantly enhance your travel experiences, making your journey more fulfilling and memorable.

In this comprehensive chapter, we will explore various strategies and techniques to help you engage in meaningful conversations with the people you meet while traveling.

1. The Importance of Effective Communication

Effective communication is crucial for building connections and understanding different cultures. It helps you:

Navigate new environments.

Gain insights into local customs and traditions.

Build friendships and networks.

Enhance your overall travel experience.

2. Preparing for Conversations

2.1 Language Skills

Learn Basic Phrases: Before you travel, learn basic phrases in the local language. Phrases like "hello," "please," "thank you," and "excuse me" can go a long way in breaking the ice.

Language Apps: Use language learning apps like Duolingo, Babbel, or Rosetta Stone to improve your language skills.

Language Exchange: Engage in language exchange programs to practice speaking and listening.

2.2 Cultural Awareness

Research Local Customs: Understand the cultural norms and etiquette of your destination. This knowledge will help you avoid potential misunderstandings and show respect for the local culture.

Be Open-Minded: Approach new cultures with an open mind and be willing to learn and adapt.

3. Starting Conversations

3.1 Icebreakers and Openers

Compliments: Complimenting someone on their outfit, accessories, or skills is a great way to start a conversation. For example, "I love your scarf! Where did you get it?"

Questions: Ask open-ended questions to encourage dialogue. Questions like "What brings you here?" or "How do you like this city?" can lead to interesting conversations.

Observations: Make a comment about your surroundings or a shared experience. For example, "This view is amazing, isn't it?" or "The food here is delicious."

3.2 Body Language

Smile: A genuine smile can make you appear friendly and approachable.

Eye Contact: Maintain eye contact to show that you are engaged and interested in the conversation.

Open Posture: Use open and relaxed body language to make others feel comfortable.

4. Sustaining Conversations

4.1 Active Listening

Pay Attention: Focus on the speaker and avoid distractions. Show that you are listening by nodding and using verbal acknowledgments like "I see" or "That's interesting."

Ask Follow-Up Questions: Asking follow-up questions shows that you are interested in what the other person is saying. For example, if someone mentions they are traveling for work, you could ask, "What kind of work do you do?"

4.2 Sharing Stories

Personal Experiences: Share your own travel experiences and stories. This not only makes the conversation more engaging but also helps build a connection through shared interests.

Humor: Use humor to lighten the mood and make the conversation more enjoyable. However, be mindful of cultural differences in humor.

4.3 Finding Common Ground

Shared Interests: Identify common interests or experiences to build rapport. Whether it's a love for hiking, food, or music, shared interests can form the basis of a strong connection.

Cultural Exchange: Share information about your own culture and be curious about theirs. This exchange can lead to enriching conversations and mutual understanding.

5. Navigating Difficult Conversations

5.1 Dealing with Language Barriers

Use Simple Language: Speak clearly and use simple language. Avoid idioms and slang that may be confusing.
Gestures and Visual Aids: Use gestures, pictures, or translation apps to help convey your message.

Patience and Understanding: Be patient and understanding if there are misunderstandings. Take your time to clarify and ensure mutual comprehension.

5.2 Handling Sensitive Topics

Avoid Controversial Subjects: Be cautious about discussing topics like politics, religion, or personal finances unless you are sure it is appropriate.

Respect Boundaries: If someone seems uncomfortable with a topic, steer the conversation in a different direction.

5.3 Conflict Resolution

Stay Calm: If a disagreement arises, stay calm and composed. Avoid raising your voice or becoming defensive.
Seek Understanding: Try to understand the other person's perspective and find common ground.

Agree to Disagree: If you cannot reach an agreement, it is okay to agree to disagree and move on to another topic.

6. Building and Maintaining Connections

6.1 Exchanging Contact Information

Social Media: Exchange social media handles or messaging app details to stay in touch.

Business Cards: If appropriate, exchange business cards for professional connections.

6.2 Following Up

Stay in Touch: Send a message or email after meeting someone to thank them for the conversation and express your desire to stay in touch.

Plan Future Meetups: If you are traveling in the same direction, plan to meet up again. This could be for a meal, a tour, or another activity.

7. Conversation Scenarios

7.1 Meeting Locals

Respectful Curiosity: Show genuine interest in learning about their culture, traditions, and daily life. Ask questions like, "What do you enjoy most about living here?"

Local Recommendations: Ask for recommendations on places to visit, eat, or things to do. This can lead to valuable insights and deeper connections.

7.2 Connecting with Fellow Travelers

Shared Experiences: Discuss your travel plans, experiences, and tips. Questions like, "What's been your favorite part of this trip so far?" can spark lively discussions.

Group Activities: Suggest group activities such as joining a tour, visiting a local attraction, or having a meal together.

7.3 Professional Networking

Common Interests: Focus on shared professional interests and experiences. Ask about their work and share your own experiences.

Opportunities for Collaboration: Discuss potential opportunities for collaboration or exchange of ideas. This can lead to meaningful professional connections.

8. Enhancing Your Social Skills

8.1 Self-Improvement

Practice Regularly: The more you practice conversing with others, the more comfortable and skilled you will become.

Reflect on Interactions: Reflect on your conversations to identify what went well and areas for improvement.

Seek Feedback: Ask trusted friends or travel companions for feedback on your social skills.

8.2 Learning from Others

Observe Skilled Conversationalists: Observe how skilled conversationalists interact and engage with others. Take note of their techniques and try to incorporate them into your own interactions.

Join Social Groups: Participate in social groups or clubs to practice your conversation skills in a supportive environment.

9. Utilizing Technology for Social Connections

9.1 Social Media and Networking Apps

Facebook Groups: Join travel-related groups to connect with other travelers and locals. Participate in discussions and meetups.

Meetup: Use the Meetup app to find and join local events and activities based on your interests.

Couchsurfing: Even if you're not staying with a host, Couchsurfing offers events and meetups for travelers and locals.

9.2 Language Exchange Apps

Tandem: Connect with language partners to practice speaking and improve your language skills.

HelloTalk: Another app for language exchange, helping you connect with native speakers around the world.

10. Embracing the Journey

10.1 Openness and Flexibility

Embrace the Unexpected: Be open to spontaneous conversations and encounters. Some of the best connections happen when you least expect them.

Adaptability: Be flexible and willing to adjust your plans to spend more time with interesting people you meet.

10.2 Positive Attitude

Stay Positive: Maintain a positive attitude and outlook. Positivity is contagious and can make you more approachable.

Enjoy the Moment: Savor the experiences and connections you make. Each interaction is an opportunity to learn and grow.

11. Reflecting on Your Experiences

11.1 Keeping a Journal

Document Interactions: Keep a journal to document your conversations and the people you meet. Reflect on what you learned and how the interactions impacted you.

Personal Growth: Reflect on how your social skills and confidence have developed over time.

11.2 Sharing Your Stories

Blogging and Social Media: Share your experiences and the stories of the people you meet through a blog or social media. This not only helps you remember the moments but also inspires others.

Cultural Exchange: Use your platform to promote cultural understanding and share the diverse perspectives you encounter.

12. Conclusion

Mastering the art of conversation while traveling can greatly enrich your experiences and help you build meaningful connections around the world.

By being prepared, open, and adaptable, you can engage in meaningful dialogues that enhance your understanding of different cultures and create lasting memories.

Remember to stay positive, embrace the unexpected, and enjoy the journey of meeting new people and forming connections that may last a lifetime.

STAYING CONNECTED AND DOCUMENTING YOUR JOURNEY

Communication Tools

Staying connected with family and friends is crucial for your safety and emotional well-being while travelling.

Here are some effective ways to keep in touch:

<u>Messaging Apps</u>

WhatsApp: Free and widely used, WhatsApp allows you to send text messages, voice messages, and make voice and video calls over the internet.

Skype: Ideal for video calls, Skype also offers text messaging and voice calls. It's a good option for staying in touch with multiple people at once through group calls.

Viber: Similar to WhatsApp, Viber offers free calls, text messaging, and multimedia sharing.

Social Media Platforms

Facebook: Share updates, photos, and videos with a broad audience. Facebook Messenger is also great for private chats.

Instagram: Ideal for sharing travel photos and stories. Instagram's direct messaging feature allows for private conversations.

Twitter/ X: Share quick updates and stay informed about news and events. This is great for finding out what's going on, quickly.

Side note: When I was in Bali, I woke up to everything shaking and the wardrobe nearly falling over. I went straight on X and looked up 'Bali', and was able to understand immediately that there was an earthquake going on, but it wasn't too serious, and I should stay put. Without X, it's likely that I wouldn't have found out the information straight away, waiting for a delayed Facebook or TikTok post, so even though I don't tend to use X day-to-day, it's actually quite a good travel tool.

Email and Blogging Platforms

Gmail/Yahoo: Email remains a reliable method for detailed communication and sharing important documents.

WordPress/Blogger: Start a travel blog to document your experiences in a more structured and detailed manner.

Blogging and Social Media

Creating a blog or maintaining an active social media presence can enrich your travel experience and provide a valuable record of your journey.

Starting a Travel Blog

Choosing a Platform: WordPress, Blogger, and Medium are popular blogging platforms. Choose one based on your technical skills and desired features.

Content Planning: Plan your content around your travels. Include stories, tips, itineraries, and personal reflections to provide a comprehensive view of your experiences.

Consistency: Regular updates keep your audience engaged. Aim to post at least once a week, depending on your travel schedule and internet access.

Social Media Strategies

Instagram: Share high-quality photos with engaging captions. Use Instagram Stories for real-time updates and behind-the-scenes content.

Facebook: Create photo albums and write detailed posts. Facebook Live is useful for sharing real-time experiences.

X: Post quick updates, travel tips, and interact with other travelers. Use hashtags to reach a broader audience.

Keeping a Journal

A personal journal is a private space to record your thoughts, feelings, and experiences. It can be a therapeutic practice and a treasured keepsake.

Types of Journals

Traditional Journal: A physical notebook where you write daily entries. Moleskine and Leuchtturm1917 offer durable, travel-friendly options. This is a nice travel present to ask for in advance, if you have well-meaning friends and family asking what you might want to take with you (and will avoid you ending up with a She-wee, which I definitely did not use).

Digital Journal: Use apps like Day One, Journey, or Evernote to keep a digital record of your travels. Digital journals can include photos, audio recordings, and GPS tagging.

Journaling Techniques

Daily Entries: Write about your daily activities, encounters, and reflections. Include details about places visited, people met, and personal thoughts.

Creative Elements: Incorporate sketches, ticket stubs, postcards, and other mementos. Use colored pens, stickers, and washi tape to personalise your journal.

Prompts and Reflections: Use prompts to inspire deeper reflection. Questions like "What was the highlight of my day?" or "How did I feel about today's experiences?" can provide meaningful insights.

Sharing Your Journey

Sharing your experiences can inspire others and create a support network. Here's how to effectively share your journey:

<u>Creating Engaging Content</u>

Stories and Anecdotes: Share personal stories that highlight unique experiences, challenges, and lessons learned.

Photos and Videos: High-quality visuals enhance your storytelling. Use editing tools like Adobe Lightroom, VSCO, or Snapseed to polish your photos.

Tips and Guides: Provide practical advice for fellow travelers. This could include packing lists, itineraries, budgeting tips, and cultural insights.

Engaging with Your Audience

Interaction: Respond to comments and messages. Engaging with your audience builds a community and enhances your reach.

Collaboration: Collaborate with other travelers, bloggers, and influencers. Guest posts, interviews, and joint projects can expand your audience.

Reflecting on Your Journey

Regular reflection helps you appreciate your experiences and learn from them. Here are some methods to facilitate reflection:

Weekly and Monthly Reviews

Review Sessions: Set aside time each week or month to review your experiences. Reflect on what you've learned, how you've grown, and any challenges you've faced.

Goal Assessment: Revisit your goals and assess your progress. Adjust your plans as needed to stay aligned with your objectives.

Deep Reflection Techniques

Mindfulness and Meditation: Practice mindfulness or meditation to stay grounded and present. Reflect on your thoughts and emotions without judgment.

Creative Outlets: Use creative outlets like drawing, painting, or writing poetry to express your reflections. Creative expression can provide deeper insights and emotional release.

Preserving Memories

Ensure your memories are preserved for years to come by creating tangible keepsakes and digital backups.

Photo Albums and Scrapbooks

Printed Albums: Create printed photo albums using services like Shutterfly, Blurb, or Mixbook. These tangible keepsakes are wonderful to look back on.

Scrapbooks: Combine photos, ticket stubs, maps, and other mementos in a scrapbook. Crafting a scrapbook can be a fun and creative way to document your journey.

Digital Backups

Cloud Storage: Use cloud storage services like Google Drive, Dropbox, or iCloud to back up your photos, videos, and documents. This ensures your memories are safe even if you lose your physical devices.

External Hard Drives: Regularly back up your data to an external hard drive for additional security.

Final Thoughts on Staying Connected

Staying connected and documenting your journey is not only about preserving memories but also about sharing your experiences and growth with others. By using the right tools and techniques, you can maintain strong connections, create lasting memories, and reflect deeply on your transformative gap year journey.

The following chapters will explore health and wellbeing while living abroad, challenges and solutions, and returning home and reflecting on your gap year experience.

CHALLENGES AND SOLUTIONS

Common Challenges

Traveling and living abroad during your gap year will undoubtedly present a variety of challenges. Recognizing and preparing for these common issues can help you navigate them more effectively.

Language Barriers

Communication Difficulties: Not knowing the local language can make everyday interactions challenging, from ordering food to asking for directions.

Cultural Nuances: Even if you have some language skills, understanding cultural nuances and idiomatic expressions can be difficult.

Cultural Differences

Culture Shock: Adjusting to a new culture can be overwhelming, with differences in customs, etiquette, and social norms.

Misunderstandings: Misunderstandings can occur due to different communication styles and cultural expectations.

Homesickness and Loneliness

Missing Home: Being away from family and friends for an extended period can lead to homesickness.

Feeling Isolated: It can be challenging to build a social network in a new country, leading to feelings of loneliness.

Financial Issues

Budgeting: Managing your finances over a long period can be difficult, especially with unexpected expenses.

Employment: Finding work abroad can be challenging, particularly if you don't have the necessary permits or language skills.

Health and Safety Concerns

Health Issues: Dealing with illness or injury in a foreign country can be daunting, especially if healthcare systems are unfamiliar.

Safety: Staying safe in unfamiliar environments requires constant vigilance and awareness.

Strategies for Overcoming Language Barriers

Learn the Basics: Before you leave, learn basic phrases and common expressions in the local language. Apps like Duolingo, Rosetta Stone, and Babbel can be very helpful.

Language Classes: Enroll in language classes once you arrive to improve your skills and meet new people.

Use Technology: Utilise translation apps like Google Translate to help with immediate communication needs.

Practice Regularly: Practice speaking with locals and don't be afraid to make mistakes. The more you use the language, the more comfortable you will become.

Adapting to Cultural Differences

Research and Prepare: Before you arrive, research the cultural norms, customs, and etiquette of your destination.

Stay Open-Minded: Approach new experiences with an open mind and a willingness to learn.

Ask Questions: If you're unsure about something, don't hesitate to ask locals for guidance. Most people appreciate the effort and are happy to help.

Observe and Adapt: Observe how locals behave in various situations and try to adapt your behaviour accordingly.

Coping with Homesickness and Loneliness

Stay Connected: Regularly communicate with family and friends back home through video calls, social media, and messaging apps.

Create a Routine: Establishing a daily routine can provide a sense of stability and normalcy.

Meet New People: Join local clubs, attend events, and participate in group activities to build a social network.

Focus on the Positive: Keep a gratitude journal to remind yourself of the positive aspects of your experience.

Managing Finances

Create a Budget: Plan a realistic budget that includes accommodation, food, transportation, activities, and an emergency fund. Use apps like Mint or YNAB to track your expenses.

Work and Volunteer: Look for part-time work, internships, or volunteer opportunities that provide free accommodation and meals.

Save Money: Cut costs by cooking your meals, using public transportation, and staying in budget accommodations.

Plan for Emergencies: Set aside an emergency fund to cover unexpected expenses.

Staying Healthy and Safe

Health Precautions: Get the necessary vaccinations before you leave and carry a basic first aid kit. Familiarize yourself with the local healthcare system and know where to find medical help.

Stay Active: Regular exercise can help you stay physically and mentally healthy. Explore local parks, join a gym, or participate in group sports.

There are lots of hotel room workouts on YouTube; even if you don't have access to a gym or park, you can still work out in your room (as long as you're not in a packed hostel dorm!)

Chances are you will meet other people who want to work out as well, and you can take group trips to a random, back-alley gym, wherever you are! I've managed to find a gym nearly everywhere I've been, and that includes the tiny Koh Lipe island in Thailand, and Gili T island off Bali.

Stay Informed: Keep up-to-date with local news and follow travel advisories. Register with your embassy or consulate.

Personal Safety: Always be aware of your surroundings and trust your instincts. Avoid risky areas, especially at night, and keep your belongings secure.

Problem-Solving Strategies

Stay Calm: When faced with a problem, take a deep breath and stay calm. Panicking will only make it harder to think clearly.

Assess the Situation: Gather as much information as possible about the problem and evaluate your options.

Seek Help: Don't be afraid to ask for help from locals, fellow travelers, or authorities. There are usually resources available to assist you.

Learn from Experience: Every challenge you face is an opportunity to learn and grow. Reflect on what you've learned and how you can apply it in the future.

Learning from Mistakes

Embrace Mistakes: Understand that making mistakes is a natural part of the learning process. Embrace them as opportunities for growth. When I was in

India, I kept saying 'chai tea', and it took a kind local to point out to me that 'chai' is tea, so I was essentially asking everyone for a 'tea tea' and looking like a right idiot in the process.

Reflect and Adjust: Reflect on what went wrong and why. Use this insight to adjust your approach and avoid similar mistakes in the future.

Stay Positive: Keep a positive attitude and remember that challenges and mistakes are temporary. Focus on the progress you're making and the lessons you're learning. It's not always easy to just 'stay positive', but practise gratitude and try and remember that at some point you might be back home, perhaps working in an office or waking up to a cold January morning, and you'll look back at at least some of your year with very fond memories.

Building Resilience

Stay Flexible: Be prepared to adapt to changing circumstances and unexpected challenges. Flexibility is key to resilience.

Stay Connected: Maintain a support network of family, friends, and fellow travelers who can offer advice and encouragement.

Practice Self-Care: Take care of your physical and mental health by eating well, exercising, and taking time to relax.

Celebrate Successes: Acknowledge and celebrate your successes, no matter how small. Recognising your achievements can boost your confidence and resilience.

By anticipating and preparing for the challenges you may face during your gap year, you can develop effective strategies to overcome them and make the most of your experience. The next chapters will cover returning home and reflecting on your gap year, as well as additional resources for further planning and support.

UNUSUAL GAP YEAR IDEAS

Taking a gap year is a fantastic opportunity to step outside your comfort zone, discover new passions, and gain experiences that will shape your future.

While many gap years involve travel and volunteering, there are countless ways to make your gap year unique and tailored to your interests.

In this chapter, we'll explore various ideas and strategies for creating a distinctive gap year experience, from alternative travel methods and creative pursuits to unusual volunteering opportunities and personal development projects.

1. Alternative Travel Methods

1.1 Overland Journeys

Traveling overland offers a slower, more immersive way to explore the world. Consider these unique overland travel experiences:

Trans-Siberian Railway: Embark on the iconic Trans-Siberian Railway, traveling from Moscow to Vladivostok or Beijing. This epic journey spans thousands of miles and offers a glimpse into the diverse cultures and landscapes of Russia, Mongolia, and China.

Cross-Country Cycling: Plan a cross-country cycling trip, such as biking from the west coast to the east coast of the United States or cycling through Europe. This physically challenging adventure allows you to connect deeply with the places you visit.

Hiking and Trekking: Undertake long-distance hikes and treks, such as the Pacific Crest Trail in the U.S., the Camino de Santiago in Spain, or the Great Himalayan Trail in Nepal. These treks provide a sense of accomplishment and a closer connection to nature.

1.2 Sail the Seas

Sailing offers a unique perspective on travel and the opportunity to visit remote locations:

Join a Sailing Crew: Learn to sail and join a crew on a yacht or sailboat. Many sailing communities are open to taking on novice sailors who are willing to learn and help out on board.

Sailing Courses: Enroll in a sailing course and obtain your sailing certification. Once certified, you can charter a boat and explore coastal regions and islands.

1.3 Road Trips and Van Life

Road trips and van life offer freedom and flexibility:

Van Conversion: Convert a van into a camper and hit the road. This allows you to travel at your own pace and stay in beautiful, off-the-beaten-path locations.

Iconic Road Trips: Plan iconic road trips, such as Route 66 in the U.S., the Great Ocean Road in Australia, or the Garden Route in South Africa.

2. Creative Pursuits

2.1 Art and Photography

Use your gap year to develop your artistic skills and capture the beauty of the world:

Art Residencies: Apply for artist residencies around the world, where you can focus on your art, collaborate with other artists, and immerse yourself in new cultures.

Photography Projects: Create a photography project documenting your travels. Consider themes such as street photography, landscapes, or portraits of people you meet.

2.2 Writing and Blogging

Share your experiences and insights through writing:

Travel Blogging: Start a travel blog to document your adventures, share tips, and inspire others. Writing regularly will help improve your writing skills and build an audience.

Creative Writing: Use your travels as inspiration for creative writing projects, such as short stories, poetry, or a novel. Attend writing workshops or retreats to hone your craft.

2.3 Music and Performing Arts

Incorporate music and performance into your gap year:

Street Performances: Perform music, dance, or other talents on the streets of the cities you visit. Street performances can help you connect with locals and other travelers.

Music Festivals: Attend and perform at music festivals around the world. This can provide exposure and networking opportunities with other musicians.

3. Unusual Volunteering Opportunities

3.1 Wildlife Conservation

Engage in unique wildlife conservation projects:

Shark Conservation: Volunteer with organizations focused on shark conservation, such as tagging and monitoring shark populations.

Elephant Sanctuaries: Work at elephant sanctuaries that focus on rescuing and rehabilitating elephants from the tourism and logging industries.

Marine Biology Research: Join marine biology research projects that study and protect marine ecosystems, such as coral reefs and sea turtle nesting sites.

3.2 Archaeological Excavations

Participate in archaeological digs and uncover history:

Ancient Civilizations: Join archaeological excavations at sites of ancient civilizations, such as the Mayan ruins in Central America, the Roman ruins in Europe, or the ancient temples in Egypt.

Field Schools: Enroll in archaeological field schools that offer hands-on training and experience in excavation techniques, artifact analysis, and site preservation.

3.3 Social Impact Projects

Make a difference in unique and impactful ways:

Community Art Projects: Collaborate on community art projects that use murals, sculptures, and other forms of art to bring communities together and address social issues.

Sustainable Development: Volunteer with organizations focused on sustainable development, such as building eco-friendly homes, promoting renewable energy, or supporting permaculture projects.

4. Personal Development and Self-Improvement

4.1 Learning New Skills

Use your gap year to acquire new skills that will benefit you personally and professionally:

Language Immersion: Spend time in a country where a language you want to learn is spoken. Enroll in language courses and practice speaking with locals daily.

Cooking Classes: Take cooking classes in different countries to learn about their culinary traditions and improve your cooking skills.

Martial Arts: Study martial arts such as Brazilian Jiu-Jitsu, Muay Thai, or Kung Fu in the countries where they originated.

4.2 Health and Wellness

Focus on your physical and mental well-being:

Yoga and Meditation Retreats: Attend yoga and meditation retreats in tranquil locations, such as the mountains of India, the beaches of Bali, or the forests of Costa Rica.

Fitness Challenges: Set fitness goals and participate in challenges such as marathons, triathlons, or endurance races in different countries.

4.3 Spiritual Exploration

Explore spiritual practices and traditions:

Monastic Retreats: Spend time in a monastery, learning about the daily life of monks and participating in their spiritual practices.

Ayahuasca Retreats: Experience traditional shamanic ceremonies in the Amazon rainforest with ayahuasca retreats, which are believed to offer profound spiritual insights.

5. Combining Travel with Education

5.1 University Exchange Programs

Participate in university exchange programs to study abroad:

Semester Abroad: Enroll in a semester abroad program through your university, allowing you to study in a different country and immerse yourself in a new academic environment.

Research Projects: Conduct research projects in collaboration with international universities, focusing on topics that interest you and contribute to your field of study.

5.2 Online Courses and Certifications

Take advantage of online learning opportunities:

MOOCs (Massive Open Online Courses): Enroll in MOOCs offered by platforms like Coursera, edX, and Udacity to learn new subjects and earn certifications.

Professional Development: Pursue professional development courses in areas such as digital marketing, project management, or coding to enhance your skills and boost your resume.

5.3 Internships and Work Placements

Gain practical experience through internships and work placements:

International Internships: Apply for internships with international companies or NGOs to gain hands-on experience in your field of interest.

Work Exchange Programs: Participate in work exchange programs like Workaway or WWOOF

(World Wide Opportunities on Organic Farms) to work in exchange for accommodation and meals.

6. Exploring Niche Interests

6.1 Adventure Sports

Focus your gap year on mastering adventure sports:

Rock Climbing: Travel to renowned climbing destinations such as Yosemite National Park in the U.S., Kalymnos in Greece, or Tonsai in Thailand to improve your climbing skills.

Surfing: Spend time in surf hotspots like Hawaii, Costa Rica, or Australia to learn or enhance your surfing abilities.

Paragliding: Take paragliding courses and fly over stunning landscapes in places like Switzerland, New Zealand, or Colombia.

6.2 Environmental Activism

Dedicate your gap year to environmental causes:

Climate Change Campaigns: Join organizations that advocate for climate change awareness and action, participating in campaigns and educational initiatives.

Eco-Communities: Live and work in eco-communities that practice sustainable living and promote environmental stewardship.

6.3 Cultural Immersion

Immerse yourself in the cultural heritage of different regions:

Traditional Crafts: Learn traditional crafts such as weaving, pottery, or woodworking from local artisans in countries like Peru, Japan, or Morocco.

Folklore and Festivals: Participate in local festivals and cultural events to experience the unique traditions and folklore of different communities.

7. Documenting Your Gap Year

7.1 Travel Blogging and Vlogging

Share your unique experiences with a wider audience:

Travel Blog: Start a travel blog to document your journey, share stories, and provide tips and insights. Use social media to promote your blog and connect with other travelers.

YouTube Channel: Create a YouTube channel to share vlogs, travel guides, and interviews with people you meet along the way.

7.2 Writing a Book

Turn your gap year experiences into a book:

Travel Memoir: Write a travel memoir that chronicles your adventures, challenges, and personal growth throughout your gap year.

Guidebook: Compile a guidebook based on your experiences, offering practical advice and insider tips for future travelers.

7.3 Photography Projects

Capture the essence of your travels through photography:

Photojournalism: Create photo essays that tell the stories of the places you visit and the people you meet.

Exhibitions: Organize exhibitions of your work in galleries or public spaces to share your perspective with a broader audience.

8. Tips for Planning a Unique Gap Year

8.1 Setting Clear Goals

Define what you want to achieve during your gap year:

Personal Goals: Identify personal goals such as learning a new language, improving your fitness, or exploring your spirituality.

Professional Goals: Set professional goals such as gaining work experience, developing new skills, or building a network.

8.2 Budgeting and Funding

Plan your finances to support your gap year activities:

Budgeting: Create a detailed budget that includes travel expenses, accommodation, food, activities, and emergency funds.

Funding Sources: Explore funding sources such as scholarships, grants, part-time work, or crowdfunding campaigns to support your gap year.

8.3 Research and Planning

Conduct thorough research and plan your itinerary:

Destinations: Research destinations that align with your interests and goals. Consider factors such as safety, cost of living, and cultural norms.

Activities: Plan activities that will help you achieve your goals and make the most of your time in each location.

8.4 Flexibility and Adaptability

Stay flexible and open to new opportunities:

Adapting Plans: Be prepared to adapt your plans based on new opportunities, unexpected challenges, or changing interests.

Embracing Spontaneity: Allow room for spontaneity and be open to unplanned adventures and experiences.

9. Making the Most of Your Unique Gap Year

9.1 Reflecting and Learning

Take time to reflect on your experiences and learn from them:

Journaling: Keep a journal to document your thoughts, feelings, and lessons learned throughout your gap year.

Self-Assessment: Regularly assess your progress towards your goals and adjust your plans as needed.

9.2 Building Connections

Focus on building meaningful connections with people you meet:

Networking: Network with professionals, fellow travelers, and locals to expand your social and professional circles.

Friendships: Form lasting friendships with people from different backgrounds and cultures.

9.3 Giving Back

Find ways to give back to the communities you visit:

Volunteering: Volunteer your time and skills to support local projects and initiatives.

Sharing Knowledge: Share your knowledge and experiences with others to inspire and support their journeys.

10. Conclusion

A unique gap year is a chance to step off the beaten path, explore your passions, and create unforgettable memories.

By considering alternative travel methods, pursuing creative interests, engaging in unusual volunteering opportunities, and focusing on personal development, you can design a gap year that is truly one-of-a-kind.

Use the tips and ideas in this chapter to plan and execute a gap year that reflects your individuality and leaves a lasting impact on your life and the lives of those you encounter.

This chapter provides a wealth of ideas and strategies for creating a unique gap year experience. By exploring alternative travel methods, creative pursuits, unusual volunteering opportunities, and personal development projects, you can design a gap year that is both enriching and memorable.

ROMANCE ON YOUR GAP YEAR

Embarking on a gap year is an exciting adventure filled with new experiences, cultures, and people. Alongside the thrill of exploration, there's a possibility of romance blooming in unexpected places.

Meeting romantic partners while traveling can add a unique dimension to your journey, creating memorable experiences and deep connections.

This chapter will guide you through navigating romance on your gap year, from meeting potential partners to managing relationships and ensuring safety.

1. Embracing the Possibility of Romance

1.1 Open Mindset

Be Open: Embrace the possibility of meeting someone special. Keep an open mind and be receptive to new connections.

Live in the Moment: Enjoy the present and focus on making genuine connections rather than seeking out romance.

1.2 Authenticity

Be Yourself: Authenticity is attractive. Be true to yourself and let potential partners get to know the real you.

Genuine Interest: Show genuine interest in others, their stories, and their backgrounds.

2. Meeting Potential Partners

2.1 Social Environments

Hostels: Hostels are social hubs where travelers from all over the world come together. Participate in hostel activities, common room gatherings, and group outings.

Tours and Activities: Join tours, excursions, and group activities to meet like-minded travelers who share your interests.

Local Events: Attend local events, festivals, and cultural activities. Engaging in local traditions can lead to meaningful connections with both travelers and locals.

2.2 Social Media and Apps

Dating Apps: Use dating apps like Tinder, Bumble, and Hinge to connect with locals and fellow travelers. Be clear about your intentions and what you're looking for.

Social Media: Join travel-related Facebook groups and follow Instagram hashtags related to your destinations. Engage with other travelers and locals online.

2.3 Language Exchange

Language Meetups: Participate in language exchange meetups to practice new languages and meet locals interested in cultural exchange.

Language Apps: Use language learning apps like Tandem or HelloTalk to connect with language partners who may also be interested in meeting up in person.

3. Navigating Romantic Relationships on the Road

3.1 Setting Boundaries and Expectations

Clear Communication: Communicate openly about your intentions, expectations, and any boundaries.

Ensure both parties are on the same page regarding the nature of the relationship.

Temporary Nature: Understand that many travel romances are temporary. Discuss how long you'll both be in the same location and what your plans are afterward.

3.2 Balancing Travel and Romance

Personal Time: Balance your time between personal travel goals and spending time with your romantic partner. Don't neglect your own interests and experiences.

Shared Experiences: Plan activities and experiences you can enjoy together, such as exploring a new city, hiking, or trying local cuisine.

3.3 Cultural Sensitivity

Respect Differences: Be mindful of cultural differences and respect local customs and traditions. This includes understanding norms around dating and public displays of affection.

Learn from Each Other: Use your relationship as an opportunity to learn about each other's cultures and perspectives.

4. Managing Long-Distance Relationships

4.1 Staying Connected

Regular Communication: Use technology to stay connected through video calls, messaging apps, and social media.

Share Experiences: Share photos, videos, and stories of your travels to keep each other updated and involved in each other's lives.

4.2 Planning Visits

Meet Up: Plan to meet up in different locations during your travels if possible. This can provide an exciting way to explore new places together.

Future Plans: Discuss future plans and possibilities for continuing the relationship after your gap year. Be realistic about the challenges and commitments involved.

4.3 Trust and Commitment

Build Trust: Trust is crucial in a long-distance relationship. Be honest and transparent to build and maintain trust.

Commitment: Evaluate your level of commitment and ensure both parties are willing to put in the effort required to make the relationship work.

5. Ensuring Safety and Well-being

5.1 Personal Safety

Public Places: When meeting someone new, always meet in public places. Inform a friend or hostel staff about your plans.

Trust Your Instincts: Trust your instincts and be cautious if something feels off. Prioritize your safety and well-being.

5.2 Safe Sex

Protection: Always use protection to prevent sexually transmitted infections (STIs) and unwanted pregnancies.

Communication: Discuss sexual health openly with your partner. Ensure both parties are comfortable and consensual.

5.3 Emotional Well-being

Self-Care: Maintain your emotional well-being by practicing self-care. Travel romances can be intense and fleeting, so take time for yourself to process your emotions.

Support Network: Stay connected with friends and family back home for emotional support and guidance.

6. Handling Breakups and Moving On

6.1 Accepting Impermanence

Embrace the Experience: Understand that many travel romances are temporary. Embrace the experience for what it was and cherish the memories.

Positive Perspective: Focus on the positive aspects and what you learned from the relationship.

6.2 Coping Strategies

Stay Busy: Keep yourself occupied with travel activities, exploring new places, and meeting new people.

Reflect and Learn: Reflect on the relationship and what you can learn from it. Use this as an opportunity for personal growth.

6.3 Staying Friends

Mutual Decision: If both parties agree, consider staying friends and maintaining a connection. This can be a positive outcome even if the romantic relationship ends.

7. Making the Most of Travel Romances

7.1 Memorable Experiences

Unique Moments: Share unique and memorable experiences with your partner, such as exploring hidden gems, trying new activities, and creating special memories.

Spontaneity: Embrace spontaneity and enjoy the thrill of new experiences together.

7.2 Learning and Growth

Cultural Exchange: Learn from each other's cultures and backgrounds. This can provide valuable insights and broaden your perspectives.

Personal Development: Use the relationship as an opportunity for personal growth and self-discovery. Reflect on how it has impacted you and what you've learned.

8. Conclusion

Meeting romantic partners and experiencing romance on your gap year can add a rich and exciting dimension to your travels.

By being open, authentic, and respectful, you can form meaningful connections that enhance your journey. Remember to prioritize your safety and well-being, communicate openly, and embrace the impermanence of travel romances.

Whether a relationship lasts for a few days or continues beyond your travels, each connection offers valuable experiences and memories that will stay with you long after your gap year ends.

GAP YEAR PROS AND CONS

Deciding to take a gap year is a significant decision that can have a profound impact on your life. To help you make an informed choice, here are the key advantages and disadvantages of taking a gap year.

Pros of Taking a Gap Year

1. Personal Growth and Development
Increased Independence: Living abroad and managing your own schedule fosters independence and self-reliance.

Self-Discovery: A gap year provides the time and space to explore your interests, passions, and strengths, helping you gain a better understanding of yourself.

2. Cultural Exposure

Cultural Immersion: Experiencing different cultures firsthand enhances cultural awareness and sensitivity.

Language Skills: Living in a foreign country is one of the best ways to learn and practice a new language, which can be a valuable asset.

3. Career Advantages

Enhanced Resume: A gap year can make your resume stand out, showing potential employers that you are adaptable, resilient, and culturally aware.

New Skills: You can develop both hard and soft skills, such as language proficiency, problem-solving, and interpersonal communication, which are highly valued in the workplace.

4. Educational Benefits

Academic Clarity: Taking a break before or during college can help clarify your academic and career goals, leading to a more focused and motivated approach to your studies.

Real-World Experience: Practical experiences gained during a gap year can complement academic learning, providing a broader perspective.

5. Lifelong Memories
Unique Experiences: A gap year offers the chance to create unforgettable memories, meet diverse people, and experience life in different parts of the world.

Friendships: The relationships you form during your travels can become lifelong connections, enriching your personal and professional network.

Cons of Taking a Gap Year

1. Financial Costs

Expense: Travelling and living abroad can be expensive, and not everyone has the financial means to support a gap year. Costs can include flights, accommodation, food, insurance, and activities.

Lost Income: Taking a gap year may mean delaying your entry into the workforce, resulting in a temporary loss of income.

2. Academic Disruption

Loss of Momentum: Taking a break from academic studies can lead to a loss of academic momentum, making it harder to return to a structured learning environment.

Delayed Graduation: A gap year may delay your graduation and subsequent entry into the job market, which can affect your career trajectory.

3. Adjustment Challenges

Reentry Adjustment: Returning home after a gap year can be challenging, as you may experience reverse culture shock and struggle to readjust to your previous lifestyle. Imagine the post-holiday blues, but times a thousand. (However, I'd never let this stop me - not doing something that might make you seriously happy, just because you'll feel miserable afterwards, is the fastest route to not actually living that you can take.)

Homesickness: Being away from family and friends for an extended period can lead to feelings of homesickness and loneliness.

4. Safety and Health Risks

Health Risks: Traveling to different countries can expose you to health risks, such as illnesses and diseases not present in your home country.

Safety Concerns: Navigating unfamiliar environments can pose safety risks, including theft, scams, and personal safety issues.

5. Uncertainty and Stress

Planning and Logistics: Organizing a gap year involves significant planning and logistics, which can be stressful and time-consuming.

Unpredictability: Unexpected challenges and uncertainties can arise, such as visa issues, travel disruptions, and cultural misunderstandings.

Weighing the Pros and Cons

When deciding whether to take a gap year, it's essential to weigh these pros and cons carefully and consider your personal circumstances, goals, and resources. Here are some questions to help guide your decision:

What are your primary motivations for taking a gap year?

Are you seeking personal growth, cultural experiences, career development, or a break from academics?

Can you afford a gap year financially?

Do you have savings, or can you find work or volunteer opportunities that cover your living expenses?

Are you prepared to handle the challenges and uncertainties of living abroad?

Do you have a support system in place to help you navigate these challenges?

How will a gap year impact your academic and career plans?

Can you defer your studies or find ways to integrate your gap year experiences into your career goals?

Conclusion

Taking a gap year is a deeply personal decision with both significant advantages and potential drawbacks. By carefully considering the pros and cons, you can make an informed choice that aligns with your personal goals and circumstances. Whether you decide to take a gap year or not, the experiences and reflections from this decision will undoubtedly contribute to your personal growth and future endeavors.

BUDGET TEMPLATE

You can create your own budget template in an Excel spreadsheet or on a piece of paper. You'll need to list categories down the left-hand-side, and then add a column for 'Estimated Cost', one for 'Actual Cost', and one for 'Notes'.

Instructions for Use:

Estimate Costs: Fill in the "Estimated Cost" column with your best guesses based on research and planning.

Track Actual Costs: As you incur expenses, fill in the "Actual Cost" column to keep track of what you're spending.
Notes: Use the "Notes" column to add any important details or reminders for each expense.

Adjust as Needed: Regularly compare estimated and actual costs. Adjust your budget and spending habits as necessary to stay on track.

Review and Reflect: At the end of each month, review your spending to see if you're meeting your budget goals and make any necessary adjustments.

Using this template, you can keep your finances organised and ensure you have a clear understanding of your spending throughout your gap year.

Categories:

International Flights
Local Transportation
Car/Bike Rentals
Travel Insurance

Hostels/Hotels
Long-term Rentals
Homestays

Eating Out
Groceries
Daily Necessities

Guided Tours
Excursions
Cultural Activities
Outdoor Activities

Vaccinations
Medical Supplies
Health Insurance

Visa Fees
Permits
Unexpected Expenses

Budget summary:
Travel Costs
Accommodation Costs
Food and Daily Living
Activity and Experience
Health and Safety
Miscellaneous

USEFUL RESOURCES

Embarking on a gap year is an exciting adventure that requires thorough planning and preparation. To help you make the most of your experience, here is a comprehensive list of useful resources, including websites, apps, organizations, and tools.

Travel Planning and Booking

Flights and Transportation

Skyscanner: A flight comparison website that helps you find the best deals on flights.

Kayak: Another popular flight search engine that also compares hotels and car rentals.

Google Flights: Useful for exploring flight options and tracking prices.

Rome2Rio: Provides comprehensive route planning, including flights, trains, buses, ferries, and driving options.

Accommodation

Booking.com: Offers a wide range of accommodations, from hostels to luxury hotels.

Hostelworld: Focused on budget accommodations, including hostels, guesthouses, and budget hotels.

Airbnb: Great for finding short-term rentals and homestays.

Couchsurfing: Connects travelers with hosts who offer free accommodation.

Travel Insurance

World Nomads: Provides travel insurance tailored for long-term travelers and adventurers.

SafetyWing: Affordable travel medical insurance designed for digital nomads and travelers.

Volunteering and Work Opportunities

Volunteering

Volunteer World: A platform that connects volunteers with projects around the world.

GoAbroad: Offers a comprehensive database of volunteer programs, internships, and study abroad opportunities.

Idealist: Lists volunteer opportunities, internships, and jobs with nonprofit organizations globally.

Work Exchanges

Workaway: Connects travelers with hosts offering free accommodation and meals in exchange for work.

WWOOF: Links volunteers with organic farms and growers needing help.

HelpX: Another work exchange platform where travelers can find work opportunities in exchange for food and accommodation.

Teaching English

TEFL.com: A resource for finding English teaching jobs abroad.

Dave's ESL Cafe: A comprehensive resource for ESL teachers, including job listings and teaching resources.

International TEFL Academy: Offers TEFL certification courses and job placement assistance.

Budgeting and Financial Management

Budgeting Tools

Mint: A free app for tracking expenses, creating budgets, and managing finances.

YNAB (You Need a Budget): Helps you create a budget and stick to it with detailed tracking and financial planning tools.

Trail Wallet: A travel expense tracker designed specifically for travellers.

Banking and Currency Exchange

TransferWise (now Wise): Offers low-cost international money transfers and a multi-currency account.

Revolut: Provides a prepaid debit card that supports multiple currencies and offers low exchange rates.

XE Currency: A reliable app for real-time currency conversion and exchange rate tracking.

Health and Safety

Health Resources

Centers for Disease Control and Prevention (CDC): Provides travel health information, including vaccination recommendations.

Travel Health Pro: Offers travel health advice, including country-specific information.

Fit for Travel: Provides information on health risks and preventive measures for travelers.

Safety Resources

Smart Traveler Enrollment Program (STEP): A free service for U.S. citizens to register their trip with the nearest U.S. embassy or consulate.

Gov.uk Foreign Travel Advice: Offers travel safety advice and updates for UK citizens.

SafeTravel (New Zealand): Provides travel safety advice and updates for New Zealanders.

Learning and Cultural Immersion

Language Learning

Duolingo: A free app for learning new languages through interactive lessons.

Rosetta Stone: Offers comprehensive language courses for a variety of languages.

Babbel: Focuses on conversation skills and practical language use.

Cultural Exchange Programs

Cultural Vistas: Offers internships, professional exchanges, and study abroad programs to foster cultural understanding.

AIESEC: Provides international volunteer and internship opportunities focused on leadership development.

Rotary Youth Exchange: Offers exchange programs for young people to experience new cultures and develop leadership skills.

Staying Connected and Documenting Your Journey

Communication Tools

WhatsApp: A free messaging and calling app for staying in touch with family and friends.

Skype: Offers video calls, voice calls, and messaging, suitable for keeping connected across distances.

Slack: Useful for staying in touch with multiple groups or project teams during your travels.

Blogging and Social Media

WordPress: A popular platform for creating blogs and websites.

Blogger: Another easy-to-use platform for starting a travel blog.

Instagram: Ideal for sharing travel photos and stories with a wide audience.

Journaling and Memory Keeping

Day One: A journaling app that allows you to document your travel experiences with text, photos, and location data.

Evernote: A versatile note-taking app that can be used for journaling, planning, and organizing travel information.
Scrapbook.com: Offers tools and supplies for creating physical scrapbooks of your travels.

Support and Networking

Expat Communities

Internations: Connects expats and global minds in various cities around the world.

Meetup: Helps you find and join groups of people with similar interests in your area.

Travel Forums and Groups

Lonely Planet Thorn Tree: A travel forum where you can ask questions and share advice with other travelers.

Reddit: Subreddits like r/travel and r/solotravel are great for advice, tips, and sharing experiences.

Alumni Networks

GoAbroad Alumni: Connects alumni of study abroad and gap year programs.

Global Nomadic: Provides a platform for alumni of their programs to stay connected and network.

Final Thoughts on Resources

Having the right resources can make your gap year planning and experience much smoother and more enjoyable. Utilise these tools and platforms to ensure you are well-prepared, stay connected, and make the most of your time abroad.

Whether it's finding the best flights, securing safe accommodation, managing your budget, or staying healthy and safe, these resources will support you every step of the way.

APPLYING FOR INTERNSHIPS ABROAD

Understanding the Benefits of Interning Abroad

Internships abroad offer a unique opportunity to gain international work experience, develop professional skills, and immerse yourself in a new culture. Here are some key benefits:

Professional Growth

Global Experience: Working in a different country provides valuable insights into international business practices and work cultures.

Skill Development: Enhance your communication, problem-solving, and adaptability skills in a global setting.

Networking: Build a network of international contacts that can support your future career.

Personal Development

Cultural Immersion: Living and working abroad allows you to experience a new culture firsthand, broadening your perspectives.

Language Skills: Improve or learn a new language through daily interactions.

Independence: Gain confidence and independence by navigating a new environment.

Researching Internship Opportunities

Finding the right internship requires thorough research. Here are some steps to help you get started:

Identifying Your Goals

Professional Goals: Define what you want to achieve professionally. Are you looking to gain experience in a specific industry or role?

Personal Goals: Consider your personal interests and how an internship abroad aligns with them. Do you want to improve language skills or explore a particular culture?

Finding Internship Programs

Online Platforms: Websites like GoAbroad, Intern Abroad HQ, and Global Experiences list international internships.

University Resources: Check with your university's career services or study abroad office for available programs and partnerships.

Professional Networks: Use LinkedIn to connect with professionals and search for internship opportunities posted by companies.

Considering Location and Logistics

Destination: Research countries and cities where you want to intern. Consider language, cost of living, and cultural aspects.

Visa Requirements: Check visa requirements for your chosen destination. Some countries offer specific visas for interns, while others might require a work visa.

Preparing Your Application

A well-prepared application can significantly increase your chances of securing an internship. Here are key steps to follow:

Crafting Your Resume

International Focus: Highlight any previous international experience or language skills.

Relevant Experience: Emphasize experiences and skills relevant to the internship role.

Clear Format: Use a clear, professional format. Tailor your resume to each application.

Writing a Cover Letter

Personalisation: Address the letter to the hiring manager and mention the specific role and company.

Motivation and Fit: Explain why you're interested in the internship and how your skills and experiences make you a good fit.

International Perspective: Highlight your interest in working abroad and any relevant international experience.

Gathering References

Professional References: Choose references who can speak to your professional skills and experiences.

Academic References: If you have limited work experience, academic references can also be valuable.

Navigating the Application Process

The application process for internships abroad can vary, but here are common steps you may encounter:

Online Applications

Application Portals: Many companies use online portals for internship applications. Follow instructions carefully and ensure all required documents are uploaded.

Deadlines: Be mindful of application deadlines. International internships may have different timelines than domestic ones.

Interviews

Preparation: Research the company and the role. Be prepared to discuss your resume, cover letter, and motivation for applying.

Cultural Awareness: Be aware of cultural differences in interview styles and expectations. For example, some cultures may value directness, while others may emphasize modesty.

Virtual Interviews: Many initial interviews may be conducted via video call. Ensure you have a stable internet connection and a quiet, professional setting.

Follow-Up

Thank You Note: Send a thank-you email after your interview, expressing appreciation for the opportunity and reiterating your interest in the role.

Follow-Up Timeline: If you haven't heard back within the expected timeline, it's acceptable to send a polite follow-up email inquiring about the status of your application.

Preparing for Your Internship Abroad

Once you've secured an internship, there are several steps to prepare for your journey:

Legal and Administrative Tasks

Visa and Work Permits: Apply for the necessary visa or work permit well in advance.

Travel Insurance: Ensure you have comprehensive travel insurance that includes health coverage.

Documentation: Gather all necessary documents, including your passport, visa, insurance details, and any paperwork from the internship provider.

Accommodation and Logistics

Housing: Research and secure accommodation. Options might include dormitories, shared apartments, or homestays.

Budgeting: Create a budget that includes accommodation, food, transportation, and leisure activities.

Local Transport: Familiarize yourself with the local transportation system and plan your daily commute.

Cultural Preparation

Cultural Research: Learn about the local culture, customs, and etiquette. This will help you adjust more quickly and avoid cultural misunderstandings.

Language Skills: If you're going to a country where the language is different, consider taking language classes or using language learning apps to improve your skills.

Making the Most of Your Internship

Maximize your internship experience by being proactive, engaged, and reflective:

Professional Conduct

Punctuality and Reliability: Always be on time and dependable in your work.

Initiative: Show initiative by seeking out additional responsibilities and offering to help with projects.

Networking: Build relationships with colleagues and other interns. Attend company events and professional gatherings.

Personal Development

Reflect on Learning: Regularly reflect on what you're learning and how it applies to your career goals.

Seek Feedback: Ask for feedback from your supervisors and colleagues to improve your performance and learn from your experiences.

Balance: Maintain a healthy work-life balance. Explore your new surroundings, engage in cultural activities, and make time for rest and relaxation.

Reflecting on Your Internship Experience

After your internship, take time to reflect on your experience and how it has contributed to your personal and professional growth:

Documenting Your Experience

Journaling: Keep a journal of your daily activities, achievements, and challenges.

Portfolio: Create a portfolio of your work, including any projects, presentations, or reports you completed.

Evaluating Your Goals

Goal Assessment: Review the goals you set before your internship. Reflect on whether you achieved them and how the experience met or differed from your expectations.

Future Planning: Consider how your internship has influenced your career aspirations and what steps you will take next.

Staying Connected

Maintain Relationships: Stay in touch with the contacts you made during your internship. Networking can provide future opportunities and support.

LinkedIn: Update your LinkedIn profile with your internship experience and connect with colleagues and supervisors.

By thoroughly preparing and actively engaging in your internship abroad, you can gain invaluable experience, develop new skills, and make lasting professional and personal connections.

HOW TO MAKE FRIENDS

One of the most enriching aspects of a gap year is the opportunity to meet new people and form lasting friendships. But it can be incredibly daunting to even think about this before you go - after all, you've got enought to prepare for without having to worry about talking to new people!

It can feel anxiety-inducing before you set off - the idea that you might have to meet new people and strike up random conversations. Trust me, it gets so, so much easier the more you travel, to the point where you're desperate to hunt out new people to hang out with, but that first step can be really scary.

Here are some strategies to help you connect with others and build a social network while traveling.

Staying in Social Accommodations

Choosing the right accommodation can greatly influence your ability to meet people.

Hostels

Social Atmosphere: Hostels are known for their friendly and communal atmosphere. Many hostels organize events, tours, and activities that make it easy to meet fellow travelers.

Shared Spaces: Common areas like lounges, kitchens, and dining rooms are perfect for striking up conversations with other guests.

Homestays

Cultural Immersion: Living with a local family provides an immersive cultural experience and often leads to deeper connections.

Family Connections: Your host family can introduce you to their friends and community, expanding your social circle.

Shared Apartments

Long-Term Connections: Renting a shared apartment with other travelers or locals can lead to strong, long-term friendships. Use platforms like Airbnb, Craigslist, or local housing boards to find shared housing.

Participating in Group Activities

Engaging in group activities is a great way to meet like-minded people.

Tours and Excursions

Day Trips: Join organized day trips and excursions. These activities often include a mix of locals and travelers, providing opportunities to make new friends.

Adventure Activities: Participate in group adventure activities like hiking, diving, or cycling tours.

Classes and Workshops

Language Classes: Enroll in language courses to improve your skills and meet other learners.

Cultural Workshops: Attend workshops on local crafts, cooking, dance, or music. These activities provide a shared experience and a common topic for conversation.

Sports and Fitness

Join a Gym: Signing up for a local gym can help you meet fitness enthusiasts.

Team Sports: Look for local sports teams or clubs. Participating in team sports like soccer, basketball, or volleyball can foster camaraderie and teamwork.

Volunteering and Working

Volunteering and working during your gap year can provide structured opportunities to meet people.

Volunteer Programs

Shared Goals: Volunteering with others who share your passion for a cause can lead to meaningful friendships.

Community Involvement: Volunteer programs often involve working with local communities, providing opportunities to build relationships with locals.

Part-Time Jobs

Work Environment: Part-time jobs in cafes, hostels, or tour companies often have a social atmosphere. Engage with your colleagues and customers to build connections.

Networking: Use your job as a platform to network with professionals and other travelers.

Internships

Professional Relationships: Internships provide a professional setting to meet people in your field of interest. Take part in office events and team projects to get to know your colleagues.

Attending Events and Meetups

Take advantage of local events and social gatherings to expand your social circle.

Cultural and Community Events

Festivals: Attend local festivals, fairs, and cultural celebrations. These events are often lively and provide a great atmosphere for meeting people.

Community Gatherings: Participate in community events such as markets, concerts, and public lectures.

Meetups and Social Apps

Meetup: Use the Meetup app to find and join groups based on your interests. Whether it's hiking, photography, or language exchange, there's likely a group for you.

Couchsurfing Events: Even if you're not staying with a host, Couchsurfing often has local events and meetups for travelers and locals.

Expat Communities

Internations: Join Internations to connect with expats in your area. They often host regular social events and gatherings.

Facebook Groups: Search for expat groups or travel communities on Facebook. These groups can be a great resource for meeting people and getting local advice.

Leveraging Technology to Connect

Technology can help bridge the gap and facilitate connections while traveling.

Social Media

Instagram and Facebook: Use social media to share your experiences and connect with other travelers. Join travel groups and participate in discussions.

Travel Blogs: Follow travel bloggers who are in your area. Engage with their content and attend any meetups they might organize.

Travel Apps

Backpackr: Connect with fellow travelers nearby who have similar travel plans.

Travello: A social network for travelers where you can share experiences and meet people on the road.

Meetup: Find local groups and events to join based on your interests.

Language Exchange Apps

Tandem: Connect with language exchange partners to practice speaking and make friends.

HelloTalk: Another app for language exchange that pairs you with native speakers around the world.

Tips for Building and Maintaining Friendships

Making friends while traveling is one thing, but maintaining those friendships requires effort and intention.

Be Open and Approachable

Positive Attitude: Approach new situations with a positive and open attitude. Smile and be friendly to those you meet.

Initiate Conversations: Don't be afraid to start conversations. Ask questions and show genuine interest in others.

Stay Connected

Exchange Contact Information: Exchange contact details with new friends and stay in touch through social media or messaging apps.

Regular Check-Ins: Keep in touch with friends you've made by regularly checking in and sharing updates about your travels.

Plan Meetups

Future Plans: If you're traveling in the same direction as a new friend, plan to meet up again later in your journey.

Reunions: Plan future reunions with friends you've made. This could be in a different country or even back home.

Be a Good Friend

Be Reliable: Follow through on plans and be reliable. Building trust is key to maintaining friendships.

Support Each Other: Offer support and be there for your friends, whether they're facing travel challenges or celebrating successes.

Final Thoughts on Making Friends

Making friends during your gap year can enrich your experience and create lasting memories. By staying open, participating in activities, and leveraging technology, you can build a network of friends from around the world. These connections can provide support, share adventures, and enhance your overall journey, making your gap year an unforgettable experience.

MENTAL HEALTH WHILE TRAVELLING

Travelling during your gap year can be an incredibly rewarding experience, but it also comes with its own set of challenges that can affect your mental health.

Here are some strategies and tips to help you maintain good mental health while on the road.

Understanding the Challenges

Common Mental Health Challenges

Homesickness: Missing family, friends, and the familiarity of home can lead to feelings of loneliness and homesickness.

Stress and Anxiety: Navigating new environments, dealing with language barriers, and managing logistics can be stressful.

Cultural Adjustment: Adapting to different cultural norms and customs can be overwhelming.

Travel Fatigue: Constant movement and the demands of travel can lead to exhaustion and burnout.

Strategies for Maintaining Mental Health

Establishing a Routine

Daily Structure: Create a daily routine that includes regular meal times, exercise, and relaxation. A routine provides stability and can reduce anxiety.

Sleep Schedule: Maintain a consistent sleep schedule. Aim for 7-9 hours of sleep per night to ensure you're well-rested.

Staying Connected with Loved Ones

Regular Check-Ins: Schedule regular calls or video chats with family and friends. Staying connected helps alleviate feelings of loneliness.

Social Media: Use social media to share your experiences and stay updated on what's happening back home.

Managing Stress and Anxiety

Mindfulness and Meditation: Practice mindfulness or meditation to manage stress. Apps like Headspace and Calm offer guided sessions that can be helpful.

Breathing Exercises: Simple breathing exercises can help calm your mind in stressful situations.

Physical Activity: Regular exercise is a powerful tool for reducing stress and improving mood. Find activities you enjoy, such as walking, yoga, or swimming.

Embracing Cultural Differences

Open Mindset: Approach new cultures with curiosity and openness. Accept that cultural differences are a natural part of travel.

Learn the Language: Learning basic phrases in the local language can enhance your interactions and reduce feelings of isolation.

Taking Care of Your Physical Health

Balanced Diet: Eat a balanced diet to ensure you have the energy and nutrients needed for your travels.

Hydration: Stay hydrated, especially in hot climates. Carry a reusable water bottle and drink water regularly.

Regular Exercise: Incorporate physical activity into your routine to boost your mood and energy levels.

Seeking Support When Needed

Recognizing When to Seek Help

Signs of Distress: Be aware of signs that you may need additional support, such as persistent sadness, anxiety, or changes in sleep and appetite.

Self-Assessment: Regularly assess your mental health and well-being. If you're struggling, don't hesitate to seek help.

Finding Mental Health Resources

Local Resources: Research mental health resources available in your destination. Many cities have counseling services and support groups for travelers and expats.

Online Counseling: Consider online counseling services like BetterHelp or Talkspace, which offer remote therapy sessions with licensed professionals.

Emergency Contacts: Know how to contact local emergency services and your country's embassy in case of a mental health crisis.

Building a Support Network

Connecting with Fellow Travelers

Travel Communities: Join travel communities and forums to connect with other travelers who understand your experiences.

Group Activities: Participate in group tours, classes, and events to meet new people and build friendships.

Engaging with Locals

Language Exchange: Engage in language exchange programs to meet locals and practice the language.

Volunteer Work: Volunteering can provide a sense of purpose and connection to the local community.

Practicing Self-Care

Taking Time for Yourself

Rest Days: Schedule regular rest days to relax and recharge. Don't feel pressured to be constantly on the move.

Hobbies and Interests: Pursue hobbies and activities that bring you joy, whether it's reading, drawing, or exploring nature.

Journaling and Reflection

Daily Journaling: Keep a journal to document your experiences and reflect on your thoughts and emotions. Journaling can be a therapeutic outlet.

Gratitude Practice: Regularly write down things you're grateful for. This practice can boost your mood and help you focus on positive aspects of your journey.

Handling Challenges and Setbacks

Developing Resilience

Problem-Solving Skills: Develop your problem-solving skills to handle unexpected challenges. Stay calm and think through solutions logically.

Positive Mindset: Maintain a positive mindset and remind yourself that setbacks are a natural part of travel. Focus on what you can learn from each experience.

Seeking Help from Others

Ask for Support: Don't be afraid to ask for help from fellow travelers, locals, or professionals when needed. Emergency Plans: Have a plan in place for emergencies, including contacts for local healthcare providers and your country's embassy.

Maintaining Long-Term Mental Health

Planning Ahead

Future Plans: Have a plan for your return home or next destination. Knowing what's next can provide a sense of stability and purpose.

Goal Setting: Set short-term and long-term goals to keep yourself motivated and focused.

Continuous Learning

Cultural Learning: Continuously learn about the cultures and places you visit. This can enhance your experience and keep your mind engaged.

Personal Growth: Reflect on your personal growth and how your travels are shaping you. Embrace the changes and challenges as part of your journey.

Final Thoughts on Mental Health

Maintaining good mental health while traveling is essential for making the most of your gap year. By being proactive, seeking support, and practicing self-care, you can navigate the challenges of travel and enjoy a fulfilling and enriching experience.

Remember that it's okay to seek help and take time for yourself. Your mental well-being is crucial to having a successful and memorable gap year.

IMPROVING YOUR IDENTITY CAPITAL

Identity capital refers to the collection of personal assets we build over time, including our skills, experiences, relationships, and knowledge.

It encompasses everything that makes us unique and valuable in both personal and professional contexts. Enhancing your identity capital during your gap year can lead to personal growth, increased self-awareness, and improved future opportunities.

This comprehensive chapter will explore various strategies and activities to help you build and enhance your identity capital.

1. Understanding Identity Capital

1.1 What is Identity Capital?

Personal Assets: Identity capital includes the skills, experiences, and knowledge you acquire over time.

These assets contribute to your sense of self and your ability to navigate different life situations.

Social Assets: It also encompasses your social networks and relationships, which can provide support, opportunities, and a sense of belonging.

1.2 Importance of Identity Capital

Personal Growth: Building identity capital helps you develop a deeper understanding of yourself, your values, and your goals.

Professional Development: It enhances your resume and makes you more attractive to potential employers or educational institutions.

Resilience: A strong sense of identity capital can make you more adaptable and resilient in the face of challenges.

2. Setting Goals for Your Gap Year

2.1 Personal Goals

Self-Discovery: Identify activities and experiences that will help you learn more about yourself.

Skill Development: Focus on acquiring new skills or improving existing ones that are important to you.

2.2 Professional Goals

Career Exploration: Use your gap year to explore different career paths and industries.

Networking: Build connections with professionals in fields that interest you.

2.3 Social Goals

Building Relationships: Form meaningful relationships with people from diverse backgrounds.

Community Involvement: Engage with local communities and contribute positively to their development.

3. Building Personal Assets

3.1 Skill Development

Language Learning: Immersing yourself in a new culture and learning a new language can enhance your communication skills and cultural understanding.

Technical Skills: Take online courses or attend workshops to gain technical skills in areas like coding, graphic design, or digital marketing.

Creative Skills: Explore your creative side through activities like writing, photography, painting, or music.

3.2 Educational Pursuits

Online Courses: Platforms like Coursera, edX, and Udacity offer courses in various subjects that can enhance your knowledge and credentials.

Workshops and Seminars: Attend workshops and seminars related to your interests or career goals.

3.3 Reflective Practices

Journaling: Keep a journal to document your experiences, thoughts, and reflections. This can help you process your experiences and track your personal growth.

Meditation and Mindfulness: Practice meditation and mindfulness to develop greater self-awareness and emotional resilience.

4. Gaining Valuable Experiences

4.1 Volunteering

Community Service: Volunteer with local organizations to support community projects and gain a sense of fulfillment.

International Programs: Participate in international volunteering programs that focus on education, healthcare, environmental conservation, or community development.

4.2 Internships and Work Experience

Professional Internships: Apply for internships in fields that interest you to gain hands-on experience and build your professional network.

Part-Time Jobs: Take on part-time jobs that allow you to develop new skills and earn money while traveling.

4.3 Travel and Cultural Immersion

Living with Locals: Stay with local families or in community-based accommodations to immerse yourself in the culture and language.

Cultural Activities: Participate in cultural activities, festivals, and events to gain a deeper understanding of the local traditions and way of life.

5. Building Social Assets

5.1 Networking

Professional Networks: Attend industry events, conferences, and networking meetups to connect with professionals in your field.

Social Media: Use platforms like LinkedIn to build and maintain professional relationships.

5.2 Forming Meaningful Relationships

Travel Companions: Connect with fellow travelers and form lasting friendships.

Local Connections: Build relationships with locals who can offer insights into their culture and way of life.

5.3 Mentorship

Finding Mentors: Seek out mentors who can provide guidance, support, and advice based on their experiences.

Being a Mentor: Share your knowledge and experiences with others, and offer mentorship to those who can benefit from your insights.

6. Leveraging Your Gap Year Experiences

6.1 Enhancing Your Resume

Documenting Achievements: Keep a record of your achievements, skills acquired, and experiences during your gap year.

Resume Writing: Highlight your gap year experiences in your resume, focusing on the skills and knowledge you gained.

6.2 Personal Branding

Online Presence: Build a professional online presence through a personal website, blog, or social media profiles.

Storytelling: Share your gap year stories and experiences in a way that reflects your personal brand and values.

6.3 Applying Skills and Knowledge

Transferable Skills: Identify transferable skills gained during your gap year and apply them to your personal and professional life.

Continuous Learning: Continue to seek opportunities for learning and growth, even after your gap year ends.

7. Overcoming Challenges

7.1 Adapting to Change

Flexibility: Be open to adapting your plans and goals as you encounter new opportunities and challenges.

Resilience: Develop resilience by learning from setbacks and using them as opportunities for growth.

7.2 Managing Finances

Budgeting: Create a budget to manage your finances effectively during your gap year.

Funding Sources: Explore funding sources such as scholarships, grants, and part-time work to support your activities.

7.3 Maintaining Balance

Work-Life Balance: Ensure a balance between work, study, and leisure activities to avoid burnout.

Self-Care: Prioritize self-care and well-being to maintain your physical and mental health.

8. Conclusion

Enhancing your identity capital during your gap year is about more than just gaining new experiences and skills; it's about developing a deeper understanding of yourself and your place in the world.

By setting clear goals, building personal and social assets, gaining valuable experiences, and leveraging your achievements, you can make the most of your gap year and set the stage for future success.

Embrace the journey, stay open to new opportunities, and continually strive for personal growth and development.

This chapter provides a comprehensive guide to enhancing your identity capital during your gap year. By focusing on personal growth, professional development, and building meaningful relationships, you can create a gap year experience that enriches your life and prepares you for future challenges and opportunities.

GAP YEAR BUCKET LIST

Creating a bucket list for your gap year can help you make the most of your time abroad and ensure you experience a variety of activities.

Here's an example gap year bucket list, including a mix of adventure, cultural immersion, personal growth, and relaxation.

Adventure and Exploration

1. Hike the Inca Trail to Machu Picchu (Peru)
Experience the stunning landscapes and ancient ruins along the way to one of the most iconic archaeological sites in the world.

2. Go on a Safari in the Serengeti (Tanzania)
Witness the incredible wildlife, including the Big Five (lion, leopard, elephant, buffalo, and rhino), in their natural habitat.

3. Dive the Great Barrier Reef (Australia)
Explore the world's largest coral reef system and marvel at its diverse marine life.

4. Trek to Everest Base Camp (Nepal)
Challenge yourself with a trek to the base camp of the world's highest peak, experiencing breathtaking views and Sherpa culture.

5. Surf in Bali (Indonesia)
Learn to surf or improve your skills on the beautiful beaches of Bali, known for its excellent waves and vibrant surf culture.

Cultural Immersion

6. Celebrate Carnival in Rio de Janeiro (Brazil)
Join the world's largest and most famous carnival, with its colorful parades, samba music, and lively atmosphere.

7. Visit the Temples of Angkor Wat (Cambodia)
Explore the vast temple complex of Angkor Wat, a UNESCO World Heritage site and a marvel of Khmer architecture.

8. Attend a Traditional Tea Ceremony in Kyoto (Japan)
Experience the elegance and tranquility of a traditional Japanese tea ceremony in the historic city of Kyoto.

9. Participate in a Homestay with a Local Family (Various Locations)

Immerse yourself in a new culture by living with a local family, learning their customs, and sharing daily life.

10. Explore the Markets of Marrakech (Morocco)
Wander through the vibrant souks of Marrakech, where you can shop for spices, textiles, and handmade crafts.

Personal Growth and Learning

11. Volunteer with a Conservation Project (Various Locations)
Contribute to wildlife or environmental conservation efforts, such as turtle rescue in Costa Rica or elephant conservation in Thailand.

12. Take a Language Immersion Course (Various Locations)
Enroll in a language school to learn a new language or improve your skills in a foreign language.

13. Teach English Abroad (Various Locations)
Share your knowledge by teaching English to students in countries like Vietnam, Spain, or China.

14. Work on an Organic Farm through WWOOF (Various Locations)
Gain hands-on experience in sustainable farming by working on an organic farm in countries like New Zealand, Italy, or Canada.

15. Complete a Professional Internship Abroad (Various Locations)
Develop your career skills and gain international work experience by interning in a field related to your studies or career goals.

Relaxation and Wellness

16. Practice Yoga at an Ashram (India)
Deepen your yoga practice and find inner peace at an ashram in India, the birthplace of yoga.

17. Spend a Week on a Remote Island (Various Locations)
Disconnect from the hustle and bustle by spending time on a remote island, such as the Maldives, Fiji, or the Greek Isles.

18. Enjoy a Thermal Spa in Iceland
Relax in the natural hot springs and geothermal spas of Iceland, such as the famous Blue Lagoon.

19. Explore the Vineyards of Tuscany (Italy)
Indulge in wine tasting and scenic vineyard tours in the picturesque region of Tuscany.

20. Attend a Silent Meditation Retreat (Various Locations)
Reconnect with yourself through a silent meditation retreat, focusing on mindfulness and self-discovery.

Unique Experiences

21. Witness the Northern Lights (Norway, Iceland, Finland)
Marvel at the natural wonder of the Aurora Borealis in the Arctic regions.

22. Take a Road Trip along the Garden Route (South Africa)
Drive along South Africa's stunning coastline, exploring national parks, beaches, and charming towns.

23. Visit the Galápagos Islands (Ecuador)
Discover the unique wildlife and ecosystems of the Galápagos Islands, which inspired Charles Darwin's theory of evolution.

24. Attend the Lantern Festival in Chiang Mai (Thailand)
Experience the magical sight of thousands of lanterns released into the sky during the annual Yi Peng Lantern Festival.

25. Ride the Trans-Siberian Railway (Russia)
Embark on an epic train journey across Russia, from Moscow to Vladivostok, experiencing diverse landscapes and cultures.

Final Thoughts on Creating Your Bucket List

Your gap year is a unique opportunity to explore the world, learn new skills, and immerse yourself in different cultures. Tailor your bucket list to your interests and goals, and be open to new experiences along the way. This list is just a starting point—add your own ideas and dreams to make your gap year truly unforgettable.

RETURNING HOME AND REFLECTING

Reverse Culture Shock

Returning home after a gap year can be just as challenging as adjusting to life abroad. You might experience reverse culture shock as you reintegrate into your home culture.

Understanding Reverse Culture Shock

Stages of Reverse Culture Shock: Similar to culture shock, reverse culture shock often involves stages such as excitement, frustration, and gradual readjustment.

Common Symptoms: These can include feeling out of place, frustration with your home culture, and difficulty reconnecting with friends and family.

Coping Strategies

Stay Connected with Your Travel Network: Keep in touch with friends you made during your gap year. Sharing experiences with those who understand can ease the transition.

Apply Your New Skills: Find ways to use the skills and knowledge you gained abroad in your daily life. This could involve volunteering, joining cultural organizations, or starting a new project.

Be Patient with Yourself: Understand that readjusting takes time. Allow yourself to feel the emotions that come with reverse culture shock and seek support if needed.

Leveraging Your Gap Year Experience

The experiences and skills gained during your gap year can be valuable assets in your academic and professional life.

Academic Integration

Reflect on Your Learning: Consider how your experiences abroad have shaped your perspectives and knowledge. This can inform your academic focus and projects.

Incorporate Your Experiences: Use your gap year experiences in assignments, presentations, and discussions. This can provide unique insights and enhance your academic work.

Pursue Related Studies: If your gap year sparked new interests, consider courses or degrees that align with these areas. Many students find their academic passions during a gap year.

Career Advancement

Update Your Resume: Highlight the skills and experiences gained during your gap year on your resume. Focus on transferable skills such as problem-solving, adaptability, and cross-cultural communication.

Discuss in Interviews: Be prepared to discuss your gap year in job interviews. Explain how it contributed to your personal and professional growth, and how it makes you a better candidate.

Network: Leverage the connections you made abroad. Join professional organizations, attend industry events, and connect with mentors who can help guide your career path.

Setting New Goals

Returning home is a great opportunity to set new personal, academic, and professional goals based on your gap year experiences.

Personal Goals

Continued Growth: Identify areas for continued personal development. This could include learning a new language, pursuing a hobby, or engaging in volunteer work.

Health and Wellbeing: Maintain the healthy habits you developed during your gap year. Regular exercise, a balanced diet, and mindfulness practices can continue to benefit you.

Academic Goals

Focused Studies: Set academic goals that reflect your new interests and perspectives. This might involve choosing a specific major, conducting research, or aiming for high academic achievement.

Extracurricular Activities: Get involved in campus activities that align with your gap year experiences, such as international clubs, language exchange programs, or study abroad organisations.

Professional Goals

Career Planning: Develop a clear career plan that incorporates your gap year experiences. Identify potential job opportunities, internships, and professional development activities.

Skill Development: Continue to build on the skills you gained during your gap year. This could involve taking additional courses, attending workshops, or obtaining certifications.

Reflecting on Your Journey

Taking time to reflect on your gap year is essential for understanding its impact on your life and integrating those experiences into your future.

Journaling and Storytelling

Write Your Story: Document your gap year journey in detail. Reflect on the highs and lows, the lessons learned, and the people who influenced you.

Share with Others: Consider sharing your experiences through a blog, social media, or public speaking. Your story can inspire others and help you process your journey.

Creating a Memory Book

Collect Memorabilia: Gather photos, ticket stubs, maps, and other memorabilia from your travels. These items can be used to create a scrapbook or memory book.

Reflective Entries: Add written reflections and anecdotes to your memory book. This can be a creative and therapeutic way to remember your experiences.

Continuous Reflection

Regular Review: Periodically review your gap year experiences and reflections. This ongoing process can provide new insights and reinforce the lessons learned.

Apply Learnings: Continuously apply the lessons and skills from your gap year to new situations. This helps solidify your growth and keeps the experience relevant in your life.

Maintaining Connections

Building and maintaining connections from your gap year can enrich your personal and professional life.

Keeping in Touch

Regular Communication: Stay in regular contact with friends and acquaintances you met during your travels. Social media, email, and messaging apps make this easy.

Reunion Plans: Plan reunions with fellow travelers. This can be a fun way to reconnect and relive shared experiences.

Networking Opportunities

Professional Connections: Use LinkedIn and other professional networks to maintain connections with colleagues, mentors, and organizations you worked with.

Alumni Networks: Join alumni networks of any programs or organisations you were part of during your gap year. These networks can provide ongoing support and opportunities.

Final Thoughts on Returning Home

Returning home after a gap year is a time of transition and reflection. By understanding the potential challenges and opportunities, you can make this period as rewarding as your time abroad. Embrace the changes, leverage your experiences, and continue to pursue growth and adventure in your everyday life.

The following chapters will provide additional resources for further planning and support, helping you maximize the benefits of your gap year experience and integrate them into your future endeavors.

THE END :)

ABOUT THE AUTHOR

Genevieve Velzian

Genevieve is a non-stop traveller, digital nomad, and lover of all things travel! She has a YouTube channel, @nomadvieve, and loves to help other people to plan their travels. She loves her Osprey rucksack, affectionately called Professor Sprout, and visiting Seven-Eleven when in Asia (it's an institution!)

Printed in Great Britain
by Amazon